AA

Pub Walks &
Cycle Rides

London

Walk routes researched and written by Rebecca Harris, Leigh Hatts, Deborah King
Cycle routes researched and written by James Hatts
Series managing editor: David Hancock

Produced by AA Publishing
© Automobile Association Developments Limited 2005
First published 2005
Reprinted 2007, 2008

Published by AA Publishing (a trading name of Automobile Association Developments Limited, whose registered office is Fanum House, Basing View, Basingstoke, Hampshire RG21 4EA; registered number 1878835).

A03749

ISBN 978-0-7495-4453-9

A CIP catalogue record for this book is available from the British Library.

The contents of this book are believed correct at the time of printing. Nevertheless, the publishers cannot be held responsible for any errors or omissions or for changes in the details given in this book or for the consequences of any reliance on the information it provides. We have tried to ensure accuracy in this book, but things do change and we would be grateful if readers would advise us of any inaccuracies they may encounter. This does not affect your statutory rights.

We have taken all reasonable steps to ensure that these walks and cycle rides are safe and achievable by people with a realistic level of fitness. However, all outdoor activities involve a degree of risk and the publishers accept no responsibility for any injuries caused to readers whilst following these walks and cycle rides. For advice on walking and cycling in safety, see pages 12 to 15.

Visit AA Publishing's website www.theAA.com/travel

Page layouts by pentacorbig, High Wycombe
Colour reproduction by Keene Group, Andover
Printed in Spain by Graficas Estella

AA

Pub Walks &
Cycle Rides

London

Locator map

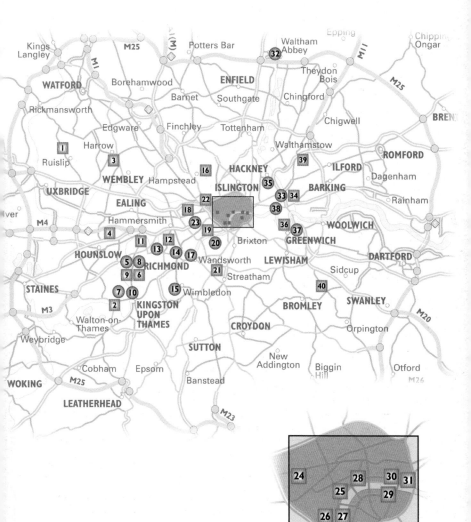

■ **Walk**

● **Cycle Ride**

–N–

0 — 5 miles
0 — 5 km

Kings Langley
M25
M1
Potters Bar
Waltham Abbey
Epping
Chipping Ongar

WATFORD
Borehamwood
ENFIELD
Theydon Bois
M11
M25

Rickmansworth
Barnet
Southgate
Chingford
BREN

Edgware
Finchley
Tottenham
Chigwell

1 Harrow
Ruislip
WEMBLEY
Hampstead
3
16
HACKNEY
ISLINGTON
Walthamstow
39
ILFORD
ROMFORD
Dagenham

UXBRIDGE
EALING
18
22
35
33 **34**
BARKING
Rainham

ver
M4
Hammersmith
23
38
36
WOOLWICH

4
19
20
Brixton
37
GREENWICH
DARTFORD

HOUNSLOW
11 **12**
13 **14** **17**
Wandsworth
LEWISHAM
Sidcup

5 **8**
RICHMOND
21
Streatham
40

STAINES
9 **6**
7 **10**
15 Wimbledon
BROMLEY
SWANLEY
M20

M3
2
KINGSTON UPON THAMES
CROYDON
Orpington

Walton-on-Thames
Weybridge
SUTTON
New Addington
Biggin Hill
Otford
M26

WOKING
M25
Cobham
Epsom
Banstead

LEATHERHEAD
M23

24
28
30 **31**
25
29
26 **27**

Contents

Picture on page 4: Mortlake on the banks of the River Thames

Contents

London

This guide includes a surprising variety of walks and rides in London and on its outskirts, easily accessible from the city. There are routes in central areas such as Putney, Fulham, Chelsea, Mayfair and Whitehall, as well as routes through the city's many parks including Regent's Park, Hyde Park and Holland Park. If the centre of town isn't for you, you could try the cycle ride from Waltham Abbey in Essex or see the deer as you walk or cycle around one of Europe's largest city parks, Richmond Park.

This being London, there are limitless places to visit, either along the way or once you have finished your walk. Attractions vary from lidos (Ruislip or Tooting Bec), through to grand houses and palaces, some managed by English Heritage or The National Trust. Routes pass Hampton Court, Osterley House, Ham House and Chiswick House. The walk with the most potential for distractions is the route along London's South Bank which passes, amongst other things, the London Eye and the Tate

Modern. Many routes have a particular theme or focus: try the parks of London, legal London, London's markets (bring your wallet!) or the old and new at the Docklands. You can even trace the route of the 1666 Great Fire of London.

As you might expect, several routes, particularly cycle rides, follow the River Thames. You can cycle along the river from attractive towns to impressive houses by going from Richmond to Ham House or from Kingston-upon-Thames to Hampton Court. Other cycles take you alongside canals such as the ride along Regent's Canal.

Many routes provide the opportunity to be in open, green spaces, where you can spot wildlife or enjoy gardens. One of the world's best-known gardens, Kew Gardens is the focus of a walk along the Thames and Holland Park has the Japanese Kyoto Garden as well as various things for children to look out for, including peacocks and large black rabbits! For the chance to see birds, head to the Wildfowl and Wetlands Trust Centre, and for open space choose between a cycle around Wimbledon Common, a walk on Hampstead Heath, or a bracing circuit of Richmond Park.

Left: The bridge over the Thames at Richmond
Below: Relaxing in Regent's Park

Using this book

Each walk and cycle ride has a coloured panel giving essential information for the walker and cyclist, including the distance, terrain, nature of the paths, and where to park your car.

1 **MINIMUM TIME:** The time stated for completing each route is the estimated minimum time that a reasonably fit family group of walkers or cyclists would take to complete the circuit. This does not allow for rest or refreshment stops.

2 **MAPS:** Each route is shown on a detailed map. However, some detail is lost because of the restrictions imposed by scale, so for this reason, we recommend that you use the maps in conjunction with a more detailed Ordnance Survey map. The relevant Ordnance Survey Explorer map appropriate for each walk or cycle is listed.

3 **START/FINISH:** Here we indicate the start location and parking area. There is a six-figure grid reference prefixed by two letters showing which 100km square of the National Grid it refers to. You'll find more information on grid references on most Ordnance Survey maps.

4 **LEVEL OF DIFFICULTY:** The walks and cycle rides have been graded simply (1 to 3) to give an indication of their relative difficulty. Easier routes, such as those with little total ascent, on easy footpaths or level trails, or those covering shorter distances are graded 1. The hardest routes, either

because they include a lot of ascent, greater distances, or are in hilly, more demanding terrains, are graded 3.

5 **TOURIST INFORMATION:** The nearest tourist information office and contact number is given for further local information, in particular opening details for the attractions listed in the 'Where to go from here' section.

6 **CYCLE HIRE:** We list, within reason, the nearest cycle hire shop/centre.

7 ❶ Here we highlight any potential difficulties or dangers along the route. At a glance you will know if the walk is steep or crosses difficult terrain, or if a cycle route is hilly, encounters a main road, or whether a mountain bike is essential for the off-road trails. If a particular route is suitable for older, fitter children we say so here.

About the pub

Generally, all the pubs featured are on the walk or cycle route. Some are close to the start/finish point, others are at the midway point, and occasionally, the recommended pub is a short drive from the start/finish point. We have included a cross-section of pubs, from homely village locals and isolated rural gems to traditional inns and upmarket country pubs which specialise in food. What they all have in common is that they serve food and welcome children.

The description of the pub is intended to convey its history and character and in the 'food' section we list a selection of dishes, which indicate the style of food available. Under 'family facilities', we say if the pub offers a children's menu or smaller portions of adult dishes, and whether the pub has a family room, highchairs, baby-changing facilities, or toys. There is detail on the garden, terrace, and any play area.

DIRECTIONS: If the pub is very close to the start point we state see Getting to the Start. If the pub is on the route the relevant direction/map location number is given, in addition to general directions. In some cases the pub is a short drive away from the finish point, so we give detailed directions to the pub from the end of the route.

PARKING: The number of parking spaces is given. All but a few of the walks and rides start away from the pub. If the pub car park is the parking/start point, then we have been given permission by the landlord to print the fact. You should always let the landlord or a member of staff know that you are using the car park before setting off.

OPEN: If the pub is open all week we state 'daily' and if it's open throughout the day we say 'all day', otherwise we just give the days/sessions the pub is closed.

FOOD: If the pub serves food all week we state 'daily' and if food is served throughout the day we say 'all day', otherwise we just give the days/sessions when food is not served.

BREWERY/COMPANY: This is the name of the brewery to which the pub is tied or the pub company that owns it. 'Free house' means that the pub is independently owned and run.

REAL ALE: We list the regular real ales available on handpump. 'Guest beers' indicates that the pub rotates beers from a number of microbreweries.

DOGS: We say if dogs are allowed in pubs on walk routes and detail any restrictions.

ROOMS: We list the number of bedrooms and how many are en suite. For prices please call the pub.

Please note that pubs change hands frequently and new chefs are employed, so menu details and facilities may change at short notice. Not all the pubs featured in this guide are listed in the *AA Pub Guide*. For information on those that are, including AA-rated accommodation, and for a comprehensive selection of pubs across Britain, please refer to the *AA Pub Guide* or see the AA's website www.theAA.com

Alternative refreshment stops

At a glance you will see if there are other pubs or cafés along the route. If there are no other places on the route, we list the nearest village or town where you can find somewhere else to eat and drink.

☛ Where to go from here

Many of the routes are short and may only take a few hours. You may wish to explore the surrounding area after lunch or before tackling the route, so we have selected a few attractions with children in mind.

Walking and cycling in safety

WALKING

All the walks are suitable for families, but less experienced family groups, especially those with younger children, should try the shorter or easier walks first. Route finding is usually straightforward, but the maps are for guidance only and we recommend that you always take the suggested Ordnance Survey map with you.

Risks

Although each walk has been researched with a view to minimising any risks, no walk in the countryside can be considered to be completely free from risk. Walking in the outdoors will always require a degree of common sense and judgement to ensure that it is as safe as possible, especially for young children.

- Be particularly careful on cliff paths and in upland terrain, where the consequences of a slip can be serious.
- Remember to check tidal conditions before walking on the seashore.
- Some sections of route are by, or cross, busy roads. Remember traffic is a danger even on minor country lanes.
- Be careful around farmyard machinery and livestock.
- Be aware of the consequences of changes in the weather and check the forecast before you set out. Ensure the whole family is properly equipped, wearing warm clothing and a good pair of boots or sturdy walking shoes. Take waterproof clothing with you and carry spare clothing and a torch if you are walking in the winter months. Remember the weather can change quickly at any time of the year, and in moorland and heathland areas, mist and fog can make route finding much harder. In summer, take account of the heat and sun by wearing a hat and carrying enough water.

- On walks away from centres of population you should carry a whistle and survival bag. If you do have an accident requiring emergency services, make a note of your position as accurately as possible and dial 999.

CYCLING

Cycling is a fun activity which children love, and teaching your child to ride a bike, and going on family cycling trips, are rewarding experiences. Not only is cycling a great way to travel, but as a regular form of exercise it can make an invaluable contribution to a child's health and fitness, and increase their confidence and sense of independence.

The growth of motor traffic has made Britain's roads increasingly dangerous and unattractive to cyclists. Cycling with children is an added responsibility and, as with everything, there is a risk when taking them out for a day's cycling. However, in recent years many measures have been taken to address this, including the on-going development of the National Cycle Network (8,000 miles utilising quiet lanes and traffic-free paths) and local designated off-road routes for families, such as converted railway lines, canal towpaths and forest tracks.

In devising the cycle rides in this guide, every effort has been made to use these designated cycle paths, or to link them with quiet country lanes and waymarked byways and bridleways. Unavoidably, in a few cases, some relatively busy B-roads have been used to link the quieter, more attractive routes.

Rules of the road
- Ride in single file on narrow and busy roads.
- Be alert, look and listen for traffic, especially on narrow lanes and blind bends and be extra careful when descending steep hills, as loose gravel can lead to an accident.
- In wet weather make sure you keep a good distance between you and other riders.
- Make sure you indicate your intentions clearly.
- Brush up on *The Highway Code* before venturing out on to the road.

Off-road safety code of conduct
- Only ride where you know it is legal to do so. It is forbidden to cycle on public footpaths, marked in yellow. The only 'rights of way' open to cyclists are bridleways (blue markers) and unsurfaced tracks, known as byways, which are open to all traffic and waymarked in red.
  - Canal towpaths: you need a permit to cycle on some stretches of towpath (www.waterscape.com). Remember that access paths can be steep and slippery and always get off and push your bike under low bridges and by locks.

- Always yield to walkers and horses, giving adequate warning of your approach.
- Don't expect to cycle at high speeds.
- Keep to the main trail to avoid any unnecessary erosion to the area beside the trail and to prevent skidding, especially if it is wet.
- Remember the Country Code.

Cycling with children

Children can use a child seat from the age of eight months, or from the time they can hold themselves upright. There are a number of child seats available which fit on the front or rear of a bike and towable two-seat trailers are worth investigating. 'Trailer bicycles', suitable for five- to ten-year-olds, can be attached to the rear of an adult's bike, so that the adult has control, allowing the child to pedal if he/she wishes. Family cycling can be made easier by using a tandem, as it can carry a child seat and tow trailers. 'Kiddy-cranks' for shorter legs can be fitted to the rear seat tube, enabling either parent to take their child out cycling. With older children it is better to purchase the right size bike rather than one that is too big, as an oversized bike will be difficult to control, and potentially dangerous.

Preparing your bicycle

A basic routine includes checking the wheels for broken spokes or excess play in the bearings, and checking the tyres for punctures, undue wear and the correct tyre pressures. Ensure that the brake blocks are firmly in place and not worn, and that cables are not frayed or too slack. Lubricate hubs, pedals, gear mechanisms and cables. Make sure you have a pump, a bell, a rear rack to carry panniers and, if cycling at night, a set of working lights.

Preparing yourself

Equipping the family with cycling clothing need not be an expensive exercise. Comfort is the key when considering what to wear. Essential items for well-being on a bike are

padded cycling shorts, warm stretch leggings (avoid tight-fitting and seamed trousers like jeans or baggy tracksuit trousers that may become caught in the chain), stiff-soled training shoes, and a wind and waterproof jacket. Fingerless gloves will add to your comfort.

A cycling helmet provides essential protection if you fall off your bike, so they are particularly recommended for young children learning to cycle.

Wrap your child up with several layers in colder weather. Make sure you and those with you are easily visible by car drivers and other road users, by wearing light-coloured or luminous clothing in daylight and reflective strips or sashes in failing light and when it is dark.

What to take with you

Invest in a pair of medium-sized panniers (rucksacks are unwieldy and can affect balance) to carry the necessary gear for you and your family for the day. Take extra clothes with you, the amount depending on the season, and always pack a light wind/waterproof jacket. Carry a basic tool kit (tyre levers, adjustable spanner, a small screwdriver, puncture repair kit, a set of Allen keys) and practical spares, such as an inner tube, a universal brake/gear cable, and a selection of nuts and bolts. Also, always take a pump and a strong lock.

Cycling, especially in hilly terrain and off-road, saps energy, so take enough food and drink for your outing. Always carry plenty of water, especially in hot and humid weather conditions. Consume high-energy snacks like cereal bars, cake or fruits, eating little and often to combat feeling weak and tired. Remember that children get thirsty (and hungry) much more quickly than adults so always have food and diluted juices available for them.

And finally, the most important advice of all—enjoy yourselves!

USEFUL CYCLING WEBSITES

NATIONAL CYCLE NETWORK

A comprehensive network of safe and attractive cycle routes throughout the UK.
It is co-ordinated by the route construction charity Sustrans with the support of more than 450 local authorities and partners across Britain.
For maps, leaflets and more information on the designated off-road cycle trails across the country contact
www.sustrans.org.uk
www.nationalcyclenetwork.org.uk

LONDON CYCLING CAMPAIGN

Pressure group that lobbies MPs, organises campaigns and petitions in order to improve cycling conditions in the capital. It provides maps, leaflets and information on cycle routes across London.
www.lcc.org.uk

BRITISH WATERWAYS

For information on towpath cycling, visit
www.waterscape.com

FORESTRY COMMISSION

For information on cycling in Forestry Commission woodland see
www.forestry.gov.uk/recreation

CYCLISTS TOURING CLUB

The largest cycling club in Britain, provides information on cycle touring, and legal and technical matters
www.ctc.org.uk

The woods and lido of Ruislip

Ruislip

MIDDLESEX

Ancient woodland contrasts with the open space of the popular lido and its enthusiastic miniature railway.

Ruislip Lido – on track for success

This is a walk of contrasts. After being cocooned along trails through the ancient woodlands that were once part of the Forest of Middlesex, the extent of the wide, flat, open space ahead when you reach the lido is impressive. Be ready for a surprise if you've never seen Ruislip Lido before – contrary to the image its name suggests, it is no longer used for swimming. It's best to do this walk on a Sunday if you plan to visit the tea rooms and the miniature railway.

The Ruislip Lido Railway began operating in 1945 with a steam locomotive called Prince Edward. At that time the line was about one third of its present length of 1.25 miles (2km). Nowadays the Ruislip Lido Railway Society operates the route. Three diesel locomotives, one steam locomotive and 15 coaches are all driven by volunteers. The railway operates all year and is one of the most successful in the south east. January, February and November are the quietest months, but numbers increase in December when special 'Santa trains' operate the 25-minute journey. The railway's ticket office is near the beach section of the lido.

A number of films have been shot here including *The Young Ones* (1961) and *Summer Holiday* (1962), both starring a youthful Cliff Richard. A couple of years earlier he had played a small part as a juvenile delinquent in the forgettable film *Serious Charge*, which nevertheless spawned his chart-topping success 'Living Doll'. But *The Young Ones*, in which Cliff

Relaxing by Ruislip Lido

played the leader of a Paddington youth club, was an enormous box-office hit and the soundtrack to the musical secured Cliff's female fanbase, remaining in the top three best-sellers for six months. The eponymous single also reached number one. Strolling around the lido today, it's difficult not to hum along to the songs of more innocent times.

the walk

1 Facing the road enter **Young Wood** to the right of the car park, by the public footpath sign, not the Area Information board. At a crossing of paths turn left over a ditch and, just before the road, cross a stile. Cross the road with care and follow the public footpath, signposted '**Hillingdon Trail**'.

2 At a **wooden post** turn left to go uphill. At a T-junction turn right, then immediately left, walking steadily downhill and over a crossing of paths. Pass through a barrier with houses visible to the wood at another T-junction.

3 Turn right along this straight track that borders **gardens**. At the end, where a road meets it on the left with a gate, turn right along a path that re-enters the woods. After 200yds (183m) turn left, taking the right fork with a pond on the right, and continue along a path that winds through the trees and ends up at a kissing gate. Take the path to the left of the gate; keep straight ahead, bearing left after another gate, and cross a brook to reach the edge of a **golf course**.

1h45 — 3.5 MILES — 5.7 KM — LEVEL 1 2 3

MAP: OS Explorer 172 Chiltern Hills East
START/FINISH: Young Wood car park off Ducks Hill Road, Ruislip; grid ref: TQ 080896
PATHS: mainly non-waymarked paths through woods
LANDSCAPE: woodland and large expanse of lido
PUBLIC TOILETS: at Ruislip Lido
TOURIST INFORMATION: Hillingdon, tel 01895 250706
THE PUB: The Water's Edge, Ruislip

Getting to the start

Young Wood car park is on the A4180 Rickmansworth road north of Ruislip. Approaching from the south (London) turn left off the A4180 into the car park. It is unmarked and if you reach the Holland and Holland Shooting Range further up the road you've gone too far.

Researched and written by:
Rebecca Harris, Deborah King

Ruislip

MIDDLESEX

4 Turn immediately right along a narrow path bordering the golf course. This path, with the golf course on the left, follows the edge of the wood. Cross a footbridge over a brook and bear right along a path that skirts the **nature reserve**.

5 Turn right over a bridge and brook into **Park Wood**. Follow this uphill and keep ahead on a reasonably straight path through the woods. You will see the track of the **miniature railway line** to the right of the wire fence.

6 Continue along this footpath as it skirts **the fence**, the miniature railway and, on the other side of this, the lido itself. Keep following the fence through the woods.

7 Turn right at the metal turnstile to the miniature railway's **ticket office**. Turn left here, along a wide path that hugs the southern end of Ruislip Lido. Continue past the children's play area and follow the path round to the right, past **The Water's Edge**

what to look for

Before you turn left at Point 8 take a detour to Poor's Field. A wide range of plants, including orchids and heather, grow here. Cattle used to drink from its two ponds. You can see the remains of a railway track, once used for carrying gravel from a nearby pit.

pub and the adjacent Woodland Centre. From the car park go through a gate and pick up the **Hillingdon Trail footpath** again across meadowland.

8 At the next footpath signpost turn left across the grass and enter **Copse Wood** by the wooden gate. Follow the footpath uphill next to a fence as it swings round to the left at the end of some fencing. The next **waymarker sign** you come to is back at Point 2. From here maintain your direction, walking ahead to retrace your footsteps back to the car park at **Young Wood** and the start.

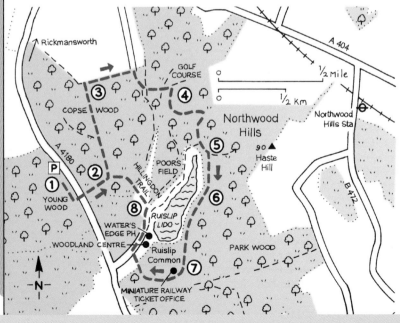

The Water's Edge

As the name suggests, the Water's Edge overlooks Ruislip Lido in a fabulous setting, with lines of picnic benches extending from the sunny terraces to the edge of the lido and nature reserve. Children will love the place as there are swans and ducks, the miniature railway chugs past the pub and the Woodland Centre is part of the pub complex. The beach at the lido is fun for adults and also has a good play area for kids. When the weather is inclement retreat inside the modern building where the large and welcoming bar and dining areas are typically kitted out with darkwood pub furnishings, and there's an indoor play area for children.

Food
The standard Brewers Fayre menu offers steaks and grills alongside pub favourites such as lasagne, steak and kidney pudding, beef and red wine casserole, salads and sandwiches.

Family facilities
The pub is really geared up for families, with play areas inside and out, a children's menu and high chairs.

Alternative refreshment stops
Choice of pubs, cafés and restaurants in Ruislip, south of the common.

☛ Where to go from here
Next to The Water's Edge pub, but only open to the public on Sunday afternoons, is the new Woodland Centre. Here you can discover a little more about the lido and surrounding woodland amid a display of old wood-cutting equipment. One of the glass cabinets contains a bundle of wood from 1812, but more up to date is the giant black-and-white poster on the wall of Cliff Richard during filming at the lido.

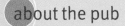
about the pub

The Water's Edge
Reservoir Road, Ruislip
Middlesex HA4 7TY
Tel: 01895 625241

DIRECTIONS: just off the A4180 north of Ruislip, beside Ruislip Common	
PARKING: plenty	
OPEN: daily; all day	
FOOD: daily	
BREWERY/COMPANY: Whitbread	
REAL ALE: none	
DOGS: not allowed	

Around Hampton Court

Discover more about the game of kings on a walk through the regal landscape of Hampton Court.

Courting a historic ball game

The majority of visitors to Hampton Court come to see the State Apartments of William III and Henry VIII, the Tudor kitchens, the maze and the 60 acres (24ha) of riverside gardens. Most miss the subtle doorway in the wall that looks like the opening to a secret garden. In fact it is the entrance to one of the more unusual parts of the palace, and the most historic court in the world – the real tennis court.

The Royal Tennis Court at Hampton Court has serious royal connections. Henry VIII played real tennis here, as did Charles I. Cardinal Wolsey built the original real tennis court in the 1520s on the site of the present Stuart court, but it remained roofless until 1636. During World War Two it was once again roofless, when a bomb hit the adjacent apartments and completely shattered the court's windows. Apart from 'real tennis', any of the terms 'royal tennis', 'court tennis' and 'close tennis' may be used to distinguish this ancient game from the more familiar 'lawn tennis' (although that is rarely played on a lawn nowadays). The game, from which many other ball games – such as table tennis and squash – are derived, was probably being played as early as the 6th century BC. The word 'tennis' stems from the French *tenez* or the Anglo-French *tenetz* which translates as 'take it', referring to what the server might call to his or her opponent. The game was very popular in France with the aristocracy, but suffered considerably for this association during the Revolution. After World War One it declined in popularity in England, but it has seen a revival lately.

If you're a real tennis novice then the court will probably look like a cross between a badminton court and a medieval street roof. Yet it's a quirky game to watch, for the serve can be over or underarm as long as the ball bounces at least once on the roof (known as a penthouse) and then on the floor within the service court. The rackets are shaped more like a buckled bicycle tyre than a conventional tennis racket, but the game is fast, energetic and skilful. The world champion, Rob Fahey, admits to having been initially attracted more by the glitzy parties than the game itself, but the sport has grown in stature over the past few years and seems now to have the ball firmly back in its own court.

the walk

1 Cross **Hampton Court Bridge**, turn right through the main gates to **Hampton Court Palace** and walk along a wide drive. Just before the palace turn left through the gatehouse and then under an **arch**.

2 Turn right just before the tea room ahead of you, then immediately left through a gate and gardens. Take the next diagonal path on the right to **Lion Gate** (signposted Formal Gardens and East Front), passing the **Maze**.

3 Go through Lion Gate and turn right to walk along the main road. Follow the wall of the estate passing **Flowerpot Gate**. Re-enter the parkland at **Paddock Gate**. Go through a wooden gate and follow the path

1h45	4.75 MILES	7.7 KM	LEVEL 1 2 3

WALK

MAP: OS Explorer 161 London South
START/FINISH: Hampton Court Railway Station. Car park in Hampton Court Road; grid ref: TQ 174697
PATHS: gravel, tarmac and riverside tracks
LANDSCAPE: landscaped grounds of historic palace
PUBLIC TOILETS: Hampton Court Park
TOURIST INFORMATION: Kingston-upon-Thames, tel 020 8547 5592
THE PUB: The King's Arms, Hampton Court
🛈 Take care near the water

Getting to the start

Hampton Court railway station is on the A309 between Esher and Sunbury, at the junction with the A3050 for Walton-on-Thames. It's easily accessed from Waterloo and Clapham Junction stations. The car park is on Hampton Court Road.

Researched and written by:
Rebecca Harris, Deborah King

Hampton Court MIDDLESEX

Top: Hampton Court Palace façade
Left: Landscaped gardens at Hampton Court

what to look for

The handsome façade of Hampton Court Palace is the nearest thing England has to Versailles, but it wasn't until Queen Victoria's reign that the gardens and maze were opened to the public. If you decide to explore the palace, allow yourself a few extra hours. Notice, too, the topiary on the gigantic yew trees leading down towards the river.

between the wall and fencing. At the end of the path go through another wooden gate and turn left through a door in the wall.

4 Turn right and bear left to walk along the railings at the bottom of the palace's **formal gardens** (by the horse carriage rides). At the **Long Wate**r, turn left and walk the length of it to the **fountains**. Turn right at the end, then first left on to a tarmac track past a pond. Bear off to the right on a grass track to skirt the edge of

Rick Pond. Go left through a metal gate, along an enclosed footpath and through a gate to reach the **River Thames**.

5 Turn left along this riverside path and follow it for 0.75 mile (1.2km) to **Kingston Bridge**. Here join the road leading to the roundabout.

6 Turn left along the main road past the roundabout. Bear left past a row of houses to enter a gate before the **Old King's Head** pub. Immediately after the cattle grid bear right along a grassy path running along the left side of the boomerang-shaped **Hampton Wick Pond**. Follow the straight path for about 0.75 mile (1.2 km) back to Hampton Court Palace and back through the door in the wall by the sign '**Hampton Court Palace and gardens**'.

7 Retrace your steps to the start, via Paddock Gate and Lion Gate (with **The King's Arms** pub on the corner).

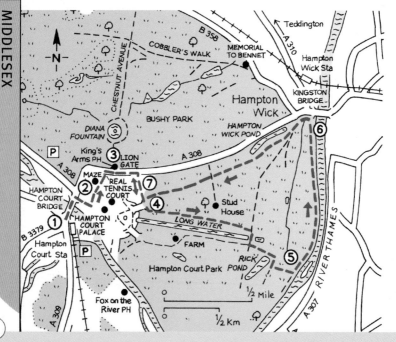

The King's Arms

Right on the edge of Hampton Court grounds, this character Georgian pub makes the ideal refreshment stop after the walk, or following a stroll around the
Hampton Court Gardens. It's cosy and comfortable inside, with plenty of oak panelling, bare brick walls, heavy beams and wooden floors topped with deep sofas, large wooden tables and an eclectic mix of furnishings. Bric-a-brac, old pictures of Hampton Court and portraits of Henry VIII's wives decorate the bars, and there's a big open fireplace with a blazing log fire in winter and a super front terrace for summer drinking. Expect a relaxed, laid-back atmosphere, excellent Badger beers and a genuine love of dogs (biscuits on the bar).*

Food

The blackboard lists a wide-ranging choice of pub food. For a snack tuck into thick-cut ham sandwiches, tomato and red onion bruschetta, or filled ciabatta rolls. For something more substantial try the steak and ale pie or lamb shank with mash, followed by strawberries and cream. There are also summer weekend barbecues and traditional Sunday roast lunches.

Family facilities

Children are very welcome in the pub.

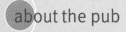

about the pub

The King's Arms
Lion Gate, Hampton Court Road,
East Molesey, London KT8 9DD
Tel: 020 8977 1729

DIRECTIONS: on the A308 between Kingston Bridge and Hampton Court Bridge, next to Lion Gate
PARKING: 7
OPEN: daily; all day
FOOD: daily; all day Saturday and Sunday
BREWERY/COMPANY: free house
REAL ALE: Badger Best, Tanglefoot & Fursty Ferret, guest beer
DOGS: welcome in the pub

Alternative refreshment stops

There is a licensed café/restaurant at the Palace. South of Hampton Court Station (0.75 mile/1.2km) in Queens Road is the Fox on the River pub, which enjoys a prime spot overlooking the River Thames.

☞ Where to go from here

Visit the famous Hampton Court Maze, which was laid out in 1714. It's quite possible to wander round this for ages, but if you want to play safe, keep to the right-hand edge going in and the left-hand one coming out. The Privy Garden has been restored with plant species from William III's day. The Great Vine, planted by 'Capability' Brown, is thought to be the oldest in the world, and is still producing grapes. Allow time to visit Henry VIII's magnificent Tudor palace. Costumed guides and audio tours bring the palace to life and provide an insight into how living conditions in the palace would have been in the time of Henry VIII and William III (www.hrp.org.uk).

Harrow-on-the-Hill

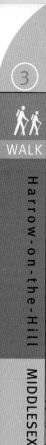

A circular walk around Harrow-on-the-Hill where Lord Byron and Anthony Trollope went to school.

Literary figures at Harrow School

From a humble start in 1572, when local farmer John Lyon obtained a royal charter, Harrow has become one of the country's best-known boys' schools. During the walk you will tread the same ground as Anthony Trollope and Lord Byron.

Lord Byron was only ten years old when he inherited his title in 1798, and he started school at Harrow in 1801. By the time he left for Cambridge University in 1805 he had no shortage of female admirers. These included Lady Caroline Lamb, with whom he had an affair. But Byron also concealed a grave secret – his father had a daughter, Augusta, from a previous marriage. Byron had met Augusta for the first time when he was only 14, but when they met again nine years later, they became close companions and she gave birth to a daughter. The following year Byron married but his wife later left him and rumours of his possible incest with Augusta soon spread. His friends and public turned against him and Byron left England. He was 36 years old when he died in Greece.

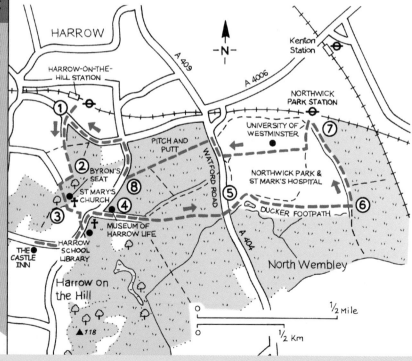

School days were not the happiest times of Anthony Trollope's life but after leaving school he joined the General Post Office (GPO). One of his achievements was to introduce the pillar box to Great Britain. By the time he decided to leave the GPO to concentrate on writing, Trollope was already an accomplished novelist – his novels including *The Warden* (1855), the 'Barsetshire' series and *The Way We Live Now* (1875).

the walk

1 Follow the signs to the left for the **Lowlands Road** exit of Harrow-on-the-Hill Station and cross the road at the pedestrian crossing. Turn left and then right, up **Lansdowne Road**. At the top of this follow the public footpath ahead, signposted **'The Hill'**.

2 Before the trees, turn right along an enclosed footpath. At a road turn left, uphill again, along a tarmac path beside a **churchyard**. (Here, you can follow the crescent-shaped path to the right and climb the steep path at the end, or continue ahead to reach St Mary's Church.)

3 Leave by the lychgate and turn right, down **Church Hill**. At the bottom turn sharp left and cross the road towards the school library and church. (For the **Castle Inn**, follow the road as it swings to the right at the bottom of Church Hill – don't turn left to go into Football Lane. Turn left down West Street. The inn is just down on the left, past a tea-shop on the right.) Follow the road as it swings to the right after the **church**.

2h00 — **3.5 MILES** — **5.7 KM** — **LEVEL 1 2 3**

MAP: OS Explorer 173 London North
START/FINISH: Harrow-on-the-Hill tube; grid ref: TQ 153880
PATHS: footpath, field and pavements
LANDSCAPE: hilltop views and buildings of Harrow School
PUBLIC TOILETS: none on route
TOURIST INFORMATION: Harrow, tel 020 8424 1103
THE PUB: Castle Inn, Harrow-on-the-Hill

Getting to the start
Harrow-on-the-Hill Station is off the A404 north of Wembley. There are pay car parks locally and meter parking in nearby streets, also Lansdowne Road. It's best accessed via the Underground, the Metropolitan Line between Aldgate and Amersham.

Researched and written by:
Rebecca Harris, Deborah King

The Old School Building at Harrow dates from 1615

4 Turn right along **Football Lane** and pick up a footpath signposted to Watford Road. At the end of the school buildings keep ahead along a path leading downhill, to reach the **playing fields**. Take a look back here at **Harrow School** and the church spires. Head towards the top left corner of the playing fields to reach a stile leading to the busy Watford Road. Cross this with care.

5 Pick up **The Ducker Footpath** opposite and carry on ahead as it passes close to Northwick Park Hospital, following it round to the left on the grass.

6 When you get to the end of the hospital buildings, turn left along a tarmac path beside a **brook**, with playing fields to your right. At the end of this long path is **Northwick Park tube**.

7 Turn left just before the tube station, along a footpath which passes two chimneys. Follow this and turn right at the tarmac road past the buildings of **Northwick Park Hospital** and the University of Westminster campus. At the end of the

footpath turn left. Cross the busy A404 at the traffic lights. Turn right to follow the dual carriageway for 100yds (91m) and go through a gate along an enclosed footpath running by the side of a **pitch-and-putt golf course**.

8 At the end of this straight, long footpath turn right along **Peterborough Road**, then left to reach Lowlands Road. **Harrow-on-the-Hill Station** is on your right.

what to look for

In the churchyard of St Mary's Church you'll notice a plaque pointing out the place where Byron loved to sit as a schoolboy. It was certainly a seat with a commanding view, looking towards Windsor. He would spend hours here, finding it the perfect place to reflect. You can see how London's suburbs have swallowed up vast areas of countryside to the north and west. In Byron's day this view would have been one of never-ending farmland and heath. Most of the sprawling development you see now dates from the earlier part of the 20th century.

The Castle

There has been a pub on the site since 1720, but the present building was rebuilt in 1901 and was the first pub to have electric lighting in Harrow. It is listed inside and out, with a wealth of original features such as open fires, smoked glass, wooden panelling and parquet flooring. Even the wallpaper is original in one of the bars. The décor is deep aubergine with sage-coloured walls, and there are thick church candles and hunting prints on the wall, while leather sofas add a more contemporary feel. All this and cracking Fuller's beers.

Food

Light lunchtime snacks range from ciabatta with hot chicken, bacon and mixed leaves to jacket potatoes with braised steak and mushrooms. Main menu meals include Thai crab cake with chilli dip, beer battered fish and chips, asparagus and beetroot risotto, and hake with paella rice and chive cream. Follow this with the raspberry cheesecake or bread and butter pudding.

about the pub

Castle Inn
30 West Street, Harrow-on-the-Hill
Middlesex HA1 3EF
Tel: 020 8422 3155

DIRECTIONS: West Street is right at the bottom of Church Hill

PARKING: none

OPEN: daily; all day

FOOD: daily; all day

BREWERY/COMPANY: Fuller's Brewery

REAL ALE: Fuller's Chiswick, London Pride, ESB

DOGS: allowed in garden on leads

Family facilities

Well-behaved children are welcome inside until 9pm; smaller portions of main dishes are available.

Alternative refreshment stops

Take a short detour along the High Street from the school library where you will find three eateries – the French Bistro, Gaucho's Pizza and Pasta, and Tea At Three, a quaint tea shop near to Harrow School's outfitters.

☛ Where to go from here

During term-time on Sundays the Museum of Harrow Life is open to the public. Although compact, it is packed with history about the school. It shows what a boy's room is like, explains about the boarding houses and their colours, famous Old Boys and the sports and activities that take place. There's also a small gift shop.

Osterley Park

Osterley

MIDDLESEX

A look at the outstanding achievements of Isambard Kingdom Brunel, whose work led to improved transport.

The age of travel

The Industrial Revolution was a period of remarkable growth. It took off in the mid-1700s, when the domestic cottage industries were gradually replaced by large factories that provided work for hundreds of people. By 1850 Britain had become the first country in the world with a predominantly industrial, urban work force. It was a time of vast development, during which Isambard Kingdom Brunel played a major role.

Brunel was born in Portsmouth in 1806, at the height of the Industrial Revolution. At that time canals were the motorways of the country. Although snail-like by today's standards, one of their great innovations had been the horse-drawn barge, because it could carry a 50-ton (53-tonne) load compared to the 300lb (136kg) capability of a horse and cart. The first section of the Grand Union Canal was opened in 1794. This walk passes two points of particular interest along it. The Hanwell Flight of six locks is an impressive 'staircase' that raises the canal 53ft (16m) in just over 600yds (549m). Three Bridges, although belonging to the railway age, also involves the canal. Here Brunel contrived a unique construction where rail, road and canal all cross each other.

Until the arrival of the railway, passenger travel was uncomfortable and very slow because the roads used by horse-drawn carriages were often uneven and muddy. But Brunel pioneered an alternative when,

together with Robert Stephenson and Joseph Locke, he helped design the world's first railway network. Brunel's contribution was the Great Western Railway between London and Bristol, a broad-gauge line that was noted for its elegant bridges, stations and viaducts. Although financed by the movement of freight, it also put long-distance passenger travel within the reach of ordinary people.

During this inspirational phase of British history Brunel also found time to design steamships, one of which became a prototype for all future ocean liners. The first, the largest ship ever built at the time, was intended to revolutionise trans-Atlantic travel in the same way that railways had transformed inland communication. His third, the Great Eastern, aimed at making a round-trip to Australia via the Cape of Good Hope without having to refuel with coal. The ship was so large that it took months to move it from its base and, unfortunately, because Australian trade slumped around this time, the project was deemed a financial flop. Despite this, the Great Eastern is remembered as the ship that laid the first successful sub-Atlantic telegraph cable, thereby hugely improving links with North America.

the walk

1 From the car park in Osterley Park, walk back along the track heading towards the **entrance gates**, passing a farm shop.

2 Just past the shop, and opposite a bungalow, turn left through a **gate** and later another, to follow a track between fields. When the path ends bear left

2h00 — **5 MILES** — **8 KM** — **LEVEL 1 2 3**

MAP: OS Explorer 161 London South

START/FINISH: Osterley Park; car park (free to National Trust members); grid ref: TQ 148779

PATHS: mixture of tow paths, tarmac paths and rough tracks

LANDSCAPE: farmland, canal boats, locks and a landscaped park

PUBLIC TOILETS: Osterley Park

TOURIST INFORMATION: Hounslow, tel 0845 456 2929

THE PUB: The Plough Inn, Norwood Green

🛈 Take care with children alongside the Grand Union Canal

through an **arch** in a brick wall, on to a grassy area. Continue in a straight line, crossing a small road ahead, more grass and down to the B454. Be careful crossing the road here (your access is hidden from traffic) and continue left to a pub, the **Hare and Hounds**.

3 Turn left along the road to pass under the M4. After a further 440yds (402m), just past a building on your left, turn right to go through a kissing gate and follow an enclosed path alongside a **playing field**. At the end of the path go through a metal gate to your right, then cross the railway line and follow the road ahead.

4 Past the bridge, go down the steps on the right to the **Grand Union Canal**, then turn right under the bridge, along the

Getting to the start

From London follow the A454 north of the A4 and turn left at the junction, following signs to Osterley House, as the B454 continues turning to the right and under the M4.

Researched and written by:
Rebecca Harris, Deborah King

tow path. In the next mile (1.6km) you will pass the **Hanwell Flight** of six locks and then Brunel's remarkable **Three Bridges** construction.

5 Cross the white bridge ahead of you and continue walking along **Melbury Avenue**. When you reach the T-junction turn left and then right at the mini-roundabout.

6 Turn left along an enclosed public footpath, signposted to St Mary's Avenue, beside **The Plough Inn**. Cross the road and continue along the footpath opposite, which crosses a field. At the far side of the field climb the steps and follow the road over the **M4 motorway**.

what to look for

Notice the sign on the white bridge just past Brunel's Three Bridges. It says: 'This bridge is insufficient to carry weights…ponderous carriages are warned against attempting to pass over this bridge'.

7 Ignoring the first metal gate along this road, turn right through the second one to re-enter **Osterley Park**. Keep going along this straight track, through farmland and an avenue of small-leaved **lime trees**, to reach a metal gate. Go past some stable buildings and the main house, then take the path around the **pond** to reach the car park where the walk began.

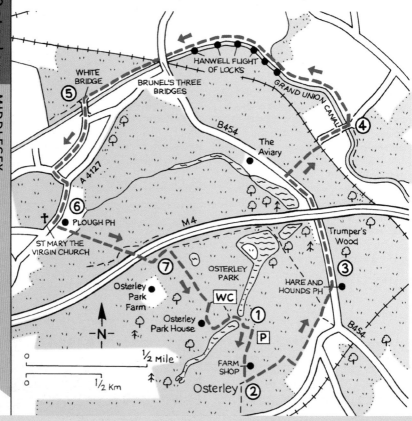

The Plough Inn

Dating from 1349, the white-painted and Grade II-listed Plough stands isolated next to a bowling green and is the oldest Fuller's pub in the country. During restoration work some wooden bricks were discovered. The landlord will show you the hook on an outside wall where, it is said, Dick Turpin used to tie his horse. Historic charm extends inside where you'll find low ceilings and genuine beams (hung with gleaming tankards), dark orange walls, darkwood pub tables and chairs, and comfortable red and green plush wall benches. On fine days, take your pint of Pride outside and enjoy the peaceful, flower-filled rear garden.

about the pub

The Plough Inn
Tentelow Road, Norwood Green
Southall, Middlesex UB22 4LG
Tel: 020 8574 1945

DIRECTIONS: beside the A4127 opposite St Mary the Virgin church (on walk at Point 6)	
PARKING: 10	
OPEN: daily; all day	
FOOD: daily	
BREWERY/COMPANY: Fuller's Brewery	
REAL ALE: Fuller's London Pride	
DOGS: welcome inside	

Osterley

MIDDLESEX

Food
The small menu offers traditional pub food, including sandwiches, omelettes, egg and chips, steak and kidney pie, and plaice and chips, along with good roast lunches on Sunday.

Family facilities
Children are welcome inside the pub, and there are swings in the garden.

Alternative refreshment stops
The Stables Tea Room in a walled garden in the stable yard at Osterley Park serves the usual array of snacks and cakes.

☞ Where to go from here
Set in 140 acres (57ha) of landscaped park and ornamental lakes, Osterley Park House is home to some of the country's best collections of work by Scottish architect, Robert Adam. It was Adam who transformed the building, which is now protected by the National Trust, into a neo-classical villa for Robert Child, a wealthy banker (www.nationaltrust.org.uk). More fine work by Robert Adam can be seen at nearby Syon House, the London home of the Duke of Northumberland, set within 200 acres (81ha) of parkland landscaped by 'Capability' Brown (www.syonpark.co.uk).

Richmond to Ham House

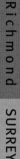

CYCLE

Richmond

SURREY

An easy riverside circuit ideal for all ages.

Ham House

Built in 1610, Ham House (see Route 9) is best remembered as home to the flamboyant Duchess of Lauderdale, whose political scheming was at the heart of Civil War politics and Restoration intrigue. Some claim that the Duchess still haunts the house today. The garden is gradually being restored to its 17th-century splendour. The Orangery houses a tea room, which offers menus inspired by the gardens, such as lavender syllabub, using lavender grown in the famous Ham cherry gardens, and locally made sausages cooked in apple and onion gravy, flavoured with sage from the Ham gardens.

Quarries once occupied the site of what is now Ham Lands Nature Reserve. These were filled in after World War Two with rubble from London buildings destroyed in the blitz. The variety of soils from all over the capital has created a unique pattern of different vegetation types attracting many unusual species.

the ride

1 From Water Lane head down the hill to the riverside. Wheel your bike along to **Richmond Bridge**. Beyond the bridge the tow path runs alongside a narrow strip of parkland parallel with **Petersham Road**. Soon **Buccleugh Gardens** is reached and the path moves briefly inland.

| 1h30 | 5.5 MILES | 8.8 KM | LEVEL 123 |

CYCLE

MAP: OS Explorer 161 London South

START/FINISH: Watermans Arms, Water Lane, Richmond; grid ref: TQ 176747

TRAILS/TRACKS: largely compacted gravel and surfaced tracks

LANDSCAPE: riverside

PUBLIC TOILETS: in Buccleugh Gardens

TOURIST INFORMATION: Richmond, tel 020 8940 9125

CYCLE HIRE: Roehampton Gate, Richmond Park, tel 07050 209249

THE PUB: Watermans Arms, Richmond

🛑 Some rough unsurfaced riverside sections

Getting to the start

The Watermans Arms is in Water Lane, a cobbled street that runs between the main post office and the river. It is approached via Red Lion Street in the town centre's one-way system. Richmond Riverside car park is just to the west of Water Lane.

Why do this cycle ride?

A fairly gentle yet fulfilling circular ride based in the busy shopping and cultural centre of Richmond, taking in the village of Ham. Discover what happened to the rubble from World War Two blitz on London.

Researched and written by: James Hatts

Richmond

SURREY

2 The path returns towards the river to skirt the edge of **Petersham Meadows**. Continue straight ahead at the **River Lane slipway**. This section of the path can be slightly rough.

3 At **Hammerton's Ferry** head inland across the boardwalk. Take the bridleway which runs alongside **Ham House**. At the end of the first section bear diagonally right to pick up **Melancholy Walk**. Look at the view back to the house behind you, then cross Sandy Lane and continue straight on till the path emerges at **Ham Common**.

Above: Following the River Thames to Richmond Hill
The Jacobean architecture of Ham House

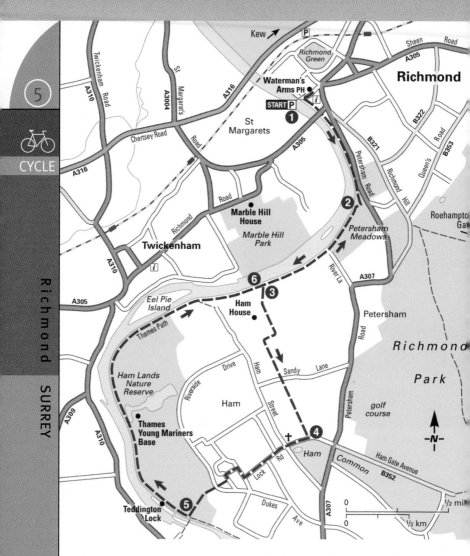

4 Turn right at **Ham Common** and keep straight ahead along Lock Road. At the end turn right into Broughton Avenue, left into Simpson Road and left into Hardwicke Road. Follow the cycle signs for the alleyway to reach Riverside Drive and the approach to **Teddington Lock**.

5 At the footbridge turn right and join the **riverside path**. Pass the locks which mark the limit of the tidal Thames. Soon you come to **Thames Young Mariners Base**; cross the bridge here and enter the **Ham Lands Nature Reserve**. Ham House is once again revealed, just past Eel Pie Island.

6 From Ham House return to **Richmond** via your outward route.

Watermans Arms

The signs in Water Lane proclaim the wonders of the Watermans all-day breakfast, but the speciality at this traditional, single-bar pub is its Thai menu. Tucked down a narrow cobbled lane leading to the Thames, it's an unpretentious little pub, noted locally for its friendly atmosphere and its genuine, unspoilt feel, and is a good place to escape the crowds that descend on the larger, more prominent riverside pubs. The décor reflects the pub's associations with the Thames – note the boat suspended from the ceiling in the bar. Arrive early in summer to secure one of the outside tables.

Food

If Thai food isn't to your taste, there's a range of burgers, chips, sandwiches and baguettes. A traditional roast is served on Sunday lunchtimes.

Family facilities

Children are welcome inside the pub.

Alternative refreshment stops

There are plenty of bars, cafés and restaurants to choose from in Richmond.

☞ Where to go from here

Visit Marble Hill House, a magnificent Thames-side Palladian villa set in 66 acres (26ha) of riverside parklands in Twickenham. It contains fine examples of early Georgian painting and furniture (www.english-heritage.org.uk). Explore the magnificent conservatories at Kew Gardens and discover plants from the world's deserts, mountains and oceans (www.kew.org). Or why not stay in Richmond and learn more about the history of the town at the Museum of Richmond (www.museumofrichmond.com).

about the pub

Watermans Arms
10 Water Lane, Richmond
Surrey TW9 1TJ
Tel: 020 8940 2893

DIRECTIONS: see Getting to the start	
PARKING: Richmond Riverside Car Park, just to the west of Water Lane	
OPEN: daily; all day	
FOOD: daily; all day	
BREWERY/COMPANY: Young's Brewery	
REAL ALE: Young's Bitter, Special & seasonal beers	

A circuit in Richmond Park

A walking safari through Europe's largest city park, Richmond Park.

Richmond Park

Richmond Park was once a royal hunting ground and, even today, it retains this upper crust image. Covering 2,500 acres (1,013ha), it is a wonderful mix of panoramic views, wildlife havens and landscaped plantations, which are worth seeing in all seasons. For the most part, the walk follows the Tamsin Trail, a 7.5-mile (12.1km) leisure path that runs around the perimeter of the park and that is for the sole use of walkers and cyclists.

The 750 or so deer are free to wander in the parkland, much of which has remained unchanged for centuries. Cars are allowed in certain areas of the park – it's not unusual for drivers to have to wait for a few minutes while a herd of deer crosses the road in front of them – but the best way to observe these beautiful creatures is on foot.

There are two types of deer in the park – red and fallow. The males and females of red deer are stags and hinds, and of fallow deer are bucks and roes. Red deer are indigenous to Britain, but fallow deer were introduced about 1,000 years ago.

Although there are enough plants to provide a nutritional diet for deer, acorns, horse chestnuts and sweet chestnuts also help to build up fat reserves during the winter months. During the rut (from September to November) the stags can often be seen fighting and herding the hinds into small breeding groups. Give them a wide berth if you pass them during the walk and keep your dog on a lead, to avoid alarming them.

If you see a bird that would look more at home in the subtropics than London, it's probably a ring-necked parakeet. These colourful birds, which have very long, pointed wings, were brought to Britain from Africa and India in the 1960s and sold as pets. Those that managed to escape began to breed successfully in the wild, and, despite the colder climate in Britain, their numbers are increasing, Noise from groups can sometimes be heard from the treetops in Richmond Park. They love to eat crab apples in summer and sycamore seeds during the rest of the year. Although they do not represent a problem to other birds, fruit growers may not be so fond of them.

the walk

1 Facing the road from the car park at **Pembroke Lodge** take the path at the far right to follow the **Tamsin Trail** in the

2h30 · **6.75 MILES** · **10.9 KM** · **LEVEL 1 2 3**

MAP:	OS Explorer 161 London South
START/FINISH:	car park at Pembroke Lodge in Richmond Park; grid ref: TQ 189728; Richmond Station (tube and rail) 1.5 miles (2.4km)
PATHS:	mainly tarmac paths
LANDSCAPE:	parkland and deer
PUBLIC TOILETS:	Pembroke Lodge
TOURIST INFORMATION:	Richmond, tel 020 8940 9125
THE PUB:	The White Cross, Richmond

🛑 Do not go close to the deer, particularly in May, June, July and October, and keep dogs on leads at this time

Getting to the start

Richmond Gate is close to the junction of the B321 and B353, a short distance off the A307 between Richmond and Kingston-upon-Thames. From Richmond station turn left into Richmond. Keep bearing left, past shops and the bridge over the river to your right. Continue up Richmond Hill to the Royal Star and Garter Home for ex-servicemen; Richmond Gate is ahead of you, leading into Richmond Park.

Researched and written by:
Rebecca Harris, Deborah King

general direction of **Ham Gate**. The path veers to the right and later runs close to the road.

2 At a crossroads leading to Ham Gate, turn left past the **Hamcross Plantation**. At the next crossroads turn right to visit the **Isabella Plantation**, otherwise continue and turn left at the next main junction, before another plantation, and circle the wood clockwise along a wide track. Bear right at the next junction and follow the path to the end of the pond.

3 Turn right along a path between the **two ponds** and continue ahead, ignoring paths branching off that would lead you to a car park. After this, turn right and follow the road that swings to the left towards

Top and right: Deer in Richmond Park

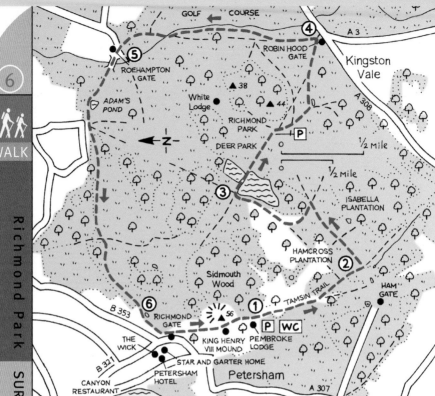

Robin Hood Gate. Deer are often spotted here but their coats give them good camouflage, especially against a background of bracken.

4 Turn left at Robin Hood Gate. Follow the gravel path of the Tamsin Trail past the Richmond Park Golf Course and on to **Roehampton Gate**.

5 Continue over a footbridge and after a further 500yds (457m), the path winds to the right of **Adam's Pond**, which is one of the watering holes used by the deer. Follow the path across the upper end of the park, past Sheen Gate, to **Richmond Gate**.

6 Turn left at **Richmond Gate** and continue along the path to reach **Pembroke Lodge** and the start of the walk.

what to look for

In the formal garden of Pembroke Lodge is the highest point in the park, Henry VIII Mound. This prehistoric burial ground is not easy to find (take the higher path past the cottage), but well worth the effort, for here is a view of the dome of St Paul's Cathedral through a keyhole of holly. The cathedral may be 10 miles (16.1km) away from the avenue of sweet chestnuts in the park, but this is better than any optical illusion, and the view is also conserved. The King was said to have stood on this mound while his second wife, Anne Boleyn, was being beheaded at the Tower of London.

The White Cross

Set right beside the Thames, the view from this Grade II-listed pub is spectacular and much admired, especially from the glorious riverside terrace on long summer evenings. Dating from 1835, it stands on the site of a former convent of Observant Friars, whose insignia was a white cross, and cleverly escapes regular flooding thanks to the monks' design of the earlier building. Inside, a central bar serves several small and cosy rooms, each filled with dark furnishings, local prints and photographs, and open fires – one fitted under a window is still lit on winter evenings. Sash windows give it an airy feel, and the views! It serves tip-top ale from Young's and a good range of wines by the glass.

about the pub

The White Cross
Water Lane, Richmond
Surrey TW9 1TH
Tel: 020 8940 6844

DIRECTIONS: from Richmond Gate head down Richmond Hill on the left-hand side. Cross the road by Richmond Bridge and take the second left, Water Lane, to find the pub by the Thames

PARKING: none

OPEN: daily; all day

FOOD: daily; lunchtimes only

BREWERY/COMPANY: Young's Brewery

REAL ALE: Young's Bitter, Special & seasonal beers

DOGS: welcome inside

Food

All food is home cooked and may include leek and potato soup, steak pie, roast pheasant with red wine sauce, lamb shanks, chilli con carne, various pastas, sausages and fish dishes. Puddings include jam sponge and apple and rhubarb crumble. Traditional Sunday roast lunches are available.

Family facilities

Children are only allowed on the terrace, where there are large umbrellas and heaters for cool evenings.

Alternative refreshment stops

The tea room at Pembroke Lodge offers hot dishes and snacks and has seating outside on the terrace in fine weather.

☞ Where to go from here

Take the tube one stop to Kew Gardens (www.kew.org) where you can lose yourself in the magnificent conservatories and discover plants from the world's deserts, mountains and oceans. Wide-open spaces, stunning vistas, wildlife and listed buildings contribute to the Gardens' unique atmosphere.

From Bushy Park to Ham

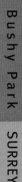

Mingle with the deer in the second largest royal park.

Cobbler's Walk

On this ride you follow Cobbler's Walk for about a mile (1.6km). The path gets its name from a memorial at the Hampton Wick Gate of Bushy Park which tells the story of local shoemaker Timothy Bennet. In 1752 he noticed that people no longer passed his shop on their way to Kingston Market from the west because they had to go the long way round by the road. Bushy Park's ranger Lord Halifax had closed the path through the park. Bennet's principle in life was that he was 'unwilling to leave the world worse than he found it' so he decided to do something about the closure of the path, and set about consulting an attorney with a view to establishing a public right of way through the park. He served notice of action on Lord Halifax, who was unimpressed with Bennet's impertinence and immediately dismissed the claim. On reflection, the earl began to see that the claim might have some foundation, and – fearing public defeat by a mere shoemaker – withdrew his opposition. As a result the pathway is enjoyed by the public to this day and now bears the name Cobbler's Walk.

the ride

1 From the car park head west past the 'no entry' signs. Remain on the **main surfaced road** when Cobbler's Walk diverges to the left. When the road turns sharply left, bear right to exit Bushy Park. Continue through the gate to reach **Hampton Road**.

2 Cross Hampton Road and pick up **King's Road** opposite, taking the first right at Connaught Road. At Gloucester

A track through Bushy Park

CYCLE

Bushy Park SURREY

3h00 · **8 MILES** · **12.9 KM** · **LEVEL 1 2 3**

MAP: OS Explorer 161 London South

START/FINISH: Bushy Park; Cobbler's Walk car park; grid ref: TQ 153701

TRAILS/TRACKS: mix of gravel paths, surfaced traffic-free trails and roads

LANDSCAPE: riverside, parkland and suburban streets

PUBLIC TOILETS: Canbury Gardens, Kingston

TOURIST INFORMATION: Kingston, tel 020 8547 5592

CYCLE HIRE: none available locally

THE PUB: The Bishop Out of Residence, Kingston-upon-Thames

🛈 Some sections shared with traffic; those with very young children may prefer to dismount

Road, turn left then right at Stanley Road. Beyond the bus stop turn left into Somerset Road, with a quick right turn into Stuart Grove, which becomes Sutherland Grove then Walpole Crescent. Turn right into Church Road to reach **Broad Street**.

3 At the traffic lights turn left to cross the railway bridge and join Teddington High Street. When the high street becomes Ferry Road look out for the **Landmark Arts Centre** on the right, housed in the imposing former St Alban's church. Cross the main road and continue along Ferry Road to the lock.

4 Dismount at the lock to cross the **double footbridges**. Once on the far bank of the river continue straight ahead to reach Riverside Drive. Cross the road and pick up the **cycle path** opposite to reach Hardwicke Road. Simpson Road and Broughton Avenue lead to Lock Road;

Getting to the start

The Cobbler's Walk car park is reached from Chestnut Avenue, which runs north–south through Bushy Park. The Park is reached from Kingston via the A308 Hampton Court Road.

Why do this cycle ride?

This ride is a voyage of discovery, from the village atmosphere of Ham Common to the market town of Kingston and the expanse of Bushy Park. Spot some of the 350 red and fallow deer in the park, introduced by Henry VIII for hunting.

Researched and written by: James Hatts

Bushy Park SURREY

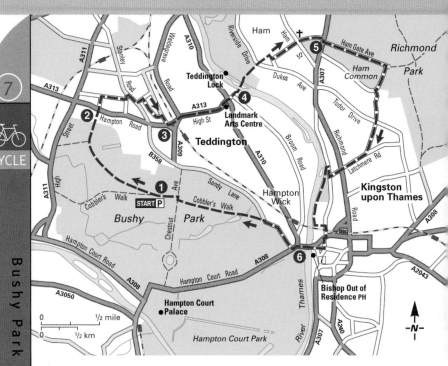

at the **Catholic church** continue straight ahead along Ham Common to reach the A307 (Upper Ham Road/Petersham Road).

5 Cross straight over (with care) into **Ham Gate Avenue**, where there is a traffic-free cycle track parallel to the road. Just before Ham Gate take a left turn down Church Road. When the road forks, bear left along Latchmere Lane. Continue for about 0.5 mile (800m) to reach Latchmere Road, bearing right to reach Richmond Road. Take care crossing here to pick up Bank Lane. At Lower Ham Road turn right to skirt the edge of Canbury Gardens and pick up the **riverside path** heading south. Just before the railway bridge head inland along Down Hall Road and follow the **signed cycle route** through Kingston town centre to cross Kingston Bridge. (For the pub, turn left down Thames Street just before the bridge, then right into Bishop Hall.)

6 Across the bridge bear left along Hampton Court Road, but take the first right along Church Grove, turning left when this joins Park Road. Enter Bushy Park through Hampton Wick Gate, and bear half-right along Cobbler's Walk, crossing Longford River with Leg-of-Mutton Pond to your left. After 0.5 mile (800m) Cobbler's Walk reaches Chestnut Avenue, a busy road running north–south across the park. Cross the avenue and pick up Cobbler's Walk diagonally opposite back to the car park.

The Bishop Out of Residence

Built in the 1960s, this is a clean and well-maintained Young's pub in a stunning location right beside the Thames with views across to Hampton

Court Park. The small riverside patio makes the most of the view and can get busy on summer weekends, so arrive early. On cooler days, take in the view from the large picture windows in the unpretentious upstairs bar. Rest your weary legs and sink into one of the deep burgundy sofas dotted around the part-carpeted, part-wood-floored room, which has a distinct sailing/rowing theme to its décor.

Food

The traditional pub menu includes various sandwiches and paninis, Cumberland sausages and mash, home-made steak and kidney pies, a range of grills and specials such as liver and bacon.

Family facilities

Children are welcome in the upstairs bar. Keep small children supervised if you are sitting outside at the waterfront tables.

about the pub

The Bishop Out of Residence
2 Bishops Hall, off Thames Street
Kingston-upon-Thames, Surrey
KT1 1QN
Tel: 020 8546 4965

DIRECTIONS: just below Kingston Bridge; see Point **5**
PARKING: Kingston Fairfield NCP near by
OPEN: daily; all day
FOOD: daily; all day
BREWERY/COMPANY: Young's Brewery
REAL ALE: Young's Bitter, Special and seasonal beers

Alternative refreshment stops

You will find a choice of pubs and cafés in Teddington High Street and in Kingston town centre.

☞ Where to go from here

Head across Bushy Park to visit Henry VIII's magnificent Tudor palace at Hampton Court. With over 500 years of royal history it has something to offer everyone, from the sumptuous, richly decorated State Apartments and beautiful gardens to the domestic reality of the Tudor kitchens. Costumed guides and fascinating audio tours bring the palace to life. Or you can explore the extensive riverside grounds which include the famous Maze, laid out in 1714 and still puzzling most who enter (www.hrp.org.uk).

Around Richmond Park

Discover the capital's largest open space and enjoy amazing views of the city.

Richmond Park

At 2,500 acres (1,012ha) Richmond Park is Europe's largest urban walled park, which has an abundance of wildlife in its varied landscape of hills, woodland gardens and grasslands. Charles I brought his court to Richmond Palace in 1625 to escape the plague in London and turned it into a park for red and fallow deer. There are more than 750 deer in the park today. Pembroke Lodge was the home of Lord Russell, prime minister in the mid-1800s. His grandson Bertrand Russell grew up here. The restaurant that now occupies the building enjoys spectacular views of the Thames Valley. The Isabella Plantation is a stunning woodland garden that was created in the early 1950s from an existing woodland and is organically run, resulting in a rich flora and fauna. Over 1,000 species of beetle have been recorded in the park. The ancient oaks provide a rich habitat for many types of insect. The park enjoys the status of a Site of Special Scientific Interest and a National Nature Reserve.

the ride

1 On entering the park at Richmond Gate look for the path on the left-hand side. (From Pembroke Lodge car park return to Richmond gate and turn right.) The path skirts **Bishops Pond**. Keep straight on past Cambrian Gate. Adam's Pond is to your right just beyond **East Sheen Gate**. The bridge over Beverley Brook means you are nearly at **Roehampton Gate**.

1h30 — **7 MILES** — **11.3 KM** — **LEVEL 1 2 3**

2 At Roehampton Gate cross the road. The path continues past the café and car park, where cycle hire is available. The **golf course** is to your left. Soon the path crosses Beverley Brook once again, then it remains between the brook and the park road as far as **Robin Hood Gate**.

3 At **Broomfield Hill** the steepest ascent of the ride awaits; signs advise cyclists to dismount. There is a bench at the top where you can recover, and a **refreshment kiosk** is just beyond. The Isabella Plantation is to your right. At **Kingston Gate** the route starts heading north.

4 At **Ham Gate** the path crosses the road and turns right, ascending

A busy stretch of the Tamsin Trail at Roe

MAP: OS Explorer 161 London South

START/FINISH: Richmond Gate at Richmond Park; grid ref: TQ 184737

TRAILS/TRACKS: largely compacted gravel

LANDSCAPE: parkland and woodland

PUBLIC TOILETS: around the park

TOURIST INFORMATION: Richmond, tel 020 8940 9125

CYCLE HIRE: Roehampton Gate, tel 07050 209249

THE PUB: Lass O'Richmond Hill, Richmond

🛈 Some short, steep climbs and a couple of longer ascents through woodland

Getting to the start

Richmond Gate is at the top of Richmond Hill (B321). You can approach from Richmond town centre or if you are coming from the south leave the A307 at Star and Garter Hill. There's parking at Pembroke Lodge in the park.

Why do this cycle ride?

This is an enjoyable circuit on an easy traffic-free trail shared with pedestrians. The stunning views of St Paul's Cathedral and other London landmarks are the only reminders that you are just 10 miles (16.1km) from the centre of the capital.

Researched and written by: James Hatts

parallel to the road. At the T-junction turn left, remaining parallel to the road. Soon the path leaves the road and opens on to a wide tree-lined avenue. As you approach **Pembroke Lodge**, glorious views of the Thames Valley unfold to the left.

5 At Pembroke Lodge the path is sometimes congested with pedestrians. Just beyond Pembroke Lodge, with the

barrow known as **King Henry VIII's mound** on your left, the cycle path unexpectedly moves to the right. At this point a marker beside the path draws attention to the incredible view of **St Paul's Cathedral**, 10 miles (16.1km) away.

6 As you ride on, a panoramic view of other London landmarks opens out. Before long you will be back at **Richmond Gate**.

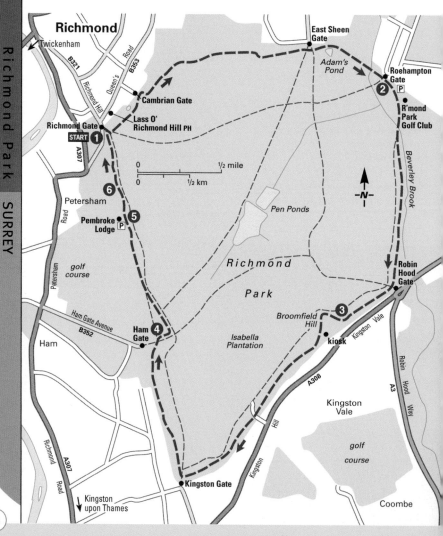

Lass O'Richmond Hill

Perched high on the steep Richmond Hill this pub is ideally placed for a cycle ride around the park. The sign outside promises 'home cooked food all day, every day, 8 days a week'. The fully air-conditioned interior means that this is a pleasant place to spend time in all weathers, and the main bar is spacious and airy. Abundant window boxes and hanging baskets add a colourful touch to the exterior. There are a few tables on the pavement, but the small garden terrace to the rear is a quieter and more pleasant place to eat and drink on sunny days.

Food

The printed menu has starters such as Wexford-style Stilton and pepper mushrooms and a duo of chicken satay and tiger prawn skewers. Main courses include roast duck with a ginger and scallion sauce and asparagus, pea and mint risotto. Banana toffee crumble and strawberry shortcake are among the puddings. There are also daily chalkboard specials.

about the pub

Lass O'Richmond Hill
8 Queens Road, Richmond
Surrey TW10 6JJ
Tel: 020 8940 1306

DIRECTIONS: on Queen's Road (B353), just to the northeast of Richmond Gate	
PARKING: 25 spaces	
OPEN: daily; all day	
FOOD: daily; all day	
BREWERY/COMPANY: Chef & Brewer	
REAL ALE: Courage Best, Fuller's London Pride	

CYCLE

Richmond Park

SURREY

Family facilities

Children are made welcome and there's a children's menu for younger family members.

Alternative refreshment stops

There are various cafés in the park and at Pembroke Lodge.

☛ Where to go from here

You're spoilt for choice for places to visit after your ride. Head off to Kew Gardens and explore some of the 3,000 acres (1,215ha) and the magnificent conservatories filled with exotic plants (www.kew.org). Take the children to Twickenham Stadium for a behind-the-scenes look at the home of England rugby and Britain's top sporting museum, the Museum of Rugby (www.rfu.com).

Along the Thames to Ham House

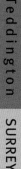

WALK

Teddington

SURREY

Following the Thames Path to Teddington Lock for views of Ham House, a fine example of Stuart architecture.

Ham House

Ham House (see Route 5), on the south bank of the Thames, is a unique example of 17th-century fashion and power. Now cared for by the National Trust (www.nationaltrust.org.uk), it has hardly changed since the Duke and Duchess of Lauderdale originally decorated it. The beautiful gardens, open all day, have been restored to their former glory and remain one of the few formal gardens that escaped the landscape trend of the 18th century. The interior is lavish, with a fine collection of period furniture, textiles and paintings, including some by Van Dyck. The gift shop sells local arts and crafts, as well as National Trust goodies, and the house puts on events for children during the holidays. There are also ghost tours and outdoor theatre. If you don't fancy the pub for lunch, there's a café with a special menu for children.

the walk

1 From the car park at Pembroke Lodge turn left to follow the **Tamsin Trail** in the direction of Richmond Gate.

Teddington Lock: a picturesque waterside scene

2h00 — **4.25 MILES** — **6.8 KM** — **LEVEL 1 2 3**

WALK

Teddington

SURREY

MAP: OS Explorer 161 London South

START/FINISH: car park at Pembroke Lodge in Richmond Park; grid ref: TQ 189728; Richmond station (tube and rail) 1.5 miles (2.4km)

PATHS: mainly tarmac paths

LANDSCAPE: parkland, woodland, riverside, views across the Thames

PUBLIC TOILETS: Pembroke Lodge

TOURIST INFORMATION: Richmond, tel 020 8940 9125

THE PUB: The New Inn, Ham Common

❶ Take care with children alongside the River Thames

Getting to the start

Richmond Gate is close to the junction of the B321 and B353, a short distance off the A307, between Richmond and Kingston-upon-Thames. From Richmond station turn left into Richmond. Keep bearing left, past shops and the bridge over the river to your right. Continue up Richmond Hill to the Royal Star and Garter Home for ex-servicemen; Richmond Gate is ahead, leading into Richmond Park.

Researched and written by:
Rebecca Harris, Deborah King

2 At Richmond Gate, walk down past the Royal Star and Garter Home. When you reach **The Wick**, a brick house with white pillars on the left, turn left into Nightingale Lane. Follow this lane as it swings to the right at the **Petersham Hotel**. When it meets Petersham Road cross to the other side by the crossing and take the path on the left, beside a brick wall. This tarmac path runs alongside **Petersham Meadows** to the River Thames.

3 Turn left and follow the path as it passes an island and, later, the nature

A gravel drive fronts Ham House, built in 1610

reserve of **Petersham Lodge Woods**. At a signpost to Ham House is the site of the **Hammerton's Ferry**, which operates all year (only at weekends in winter). Continue past Eel Pie Island and on to Ham Lands, a wooded local nature reserve. Turn left just before the blue bridge at **Teddington Lock**.

4 Cross over two roads and pass through a set of metal gates to go along a fenced footpath. At the end turn right, then take the first left into Lock Road. Continue ahead over a junction along **The Common** (here a road), past a pond. Just before the road bends to the right, and after the last cottage on the left, is a **white fence**.

5 Beside this fence is **Melancholy Walk**, a long, gravel path leading to Ham House, seen through a tunnel of trees. Continue along The Common, to **The New Inn** pub on the corner of the road junction. Cross at the pedestrian lights on to Ham Gate Avenue. Follow this all the way back to Richmond Park, to reach the Tamsin Trail and turn left back along the Trail to **Pembroke Lodge** and the car park.

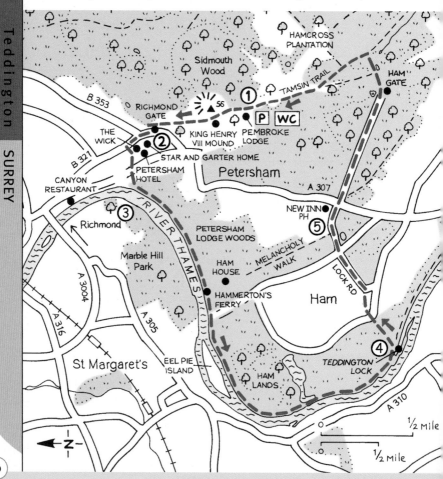

The New Inn

The Georgian, brick-built New Inn is in an attractive spot on Ham Common, close to Richmond Park and Ham House. The classic pub interior has comfortable banquette seating, a wood-panelled bar, traditional dark wood tables and chairs, beamed ceilings and cosy corners close to warming winter log fires. It's particularly lovely in summer, with picnic tables and tubs of flowers on a pretty front terrace, with further al fresco seating on a quieter rear terrace. Children and dogs are welcome, the latter provided with water bowls. Well-kept real ales, friendly service, a village local atmosphere and freshly prepared pub food add to the enjoyment.

Food

For a light meal choose from a range of ciabatta sandwiches, paninis or filled jacket potatoes. The menu includes warm chorizo, smoked bacon and tomato salad, cod and chips, seared tuna steak with citrus butter, and rib-eye steak with pepper sauce. Daily specials and a choice of Sunday roast lunches are also available.

Family facilities

Children are welcome inside until 6pm. Smaller portions of adult dishes are available and there are baby-changing facilities in the toilets.

Alternative refreshment stops

The tea room at Pembroke Lodge offers hot dishes and snacks and has seating outside on the terrace in fine weather.

☛ Where to go from here

A tour of Twickenham rugby stadium includes a visit to the England dressing room and magnificent views of the stadium from the top of the north stand. At the Museum of Rugby, interactive displays, period set pieces and video footage bring the history of the game to life (www.rfu.com).

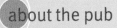

about the pub

The New Inn
345 Petersham Road, Ham Common
Richmond, Surrey TW10 7DD
Tel: 020 8940 9444

DIRECTIONS: beside the A307 (Petersham Road) between Richmond and Kingston-upon-Thames (on walk just after Point **5**)

PARKING: plenty

OPEN: daily; all day

FOOD: daily; all day

BREWERY/COMPANY: free house

REAL ALE: Young's Bitter, Greene King Abbot Ale, Adnams Broadside, guest beer

DOGS: allowed inside the pub

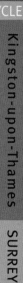
Kingston-upon-Thames to Hampton Court

A traffic-free riverside ride to one of Britain's most famous royal palaces.

Hampton Court Palace

The palace is often associated with Henry VIII, who in just ten years spent more than £62,000 (equivalent to £18 million today) rebuilding and extending Hampton Court. At the time of his death, Henry had more than 60 houses and Hampton Court was his fourth favourite; he spent 811 days here during his 38-year reign, and all of his six wives came to the palace. The story of Hampton Court goes back to the early

Above: Kingston Bridge
Left: Traffic-free cycling

2h00 **7 MILES** **11.3 KM** **LEVEL 1 2 3**

1200s, when the site was first occupied by the Knights Hospitallers of St John of Jerusalem. For another royal occupant of the palace, however, it was later to become a prison – Charles I was held here for three months. George II was the last monarch to use the palace fully; his heir George III didn't much care for Hampton Court, remarking after a fire in some outbuildings that he 'should not have been sorry if it had burnt down'. The palace was opened to the public by Queen Victoria in 1838. Today, besides the palace itself, the world-famous maze and the Great Vine (planted in 1768) continue to delight thousands of visitors every year.

the ride

1 From **The Boaters Inn** turn south along the shady riverside path. Just before the railway bridge follow the **signed cycle route** to the left along Down Hall Road. Turn right at Skerne Road and follow the cycle track under the railway bridge. Use the cycle crossing provided to cross **Wood Street**. Take the buses-and-cyclists-only section of Wood Street round the side of the Bentall Centre, following round to reach the crossroads with Clarence Street. Turn right to approach **Kingston Bridge** using the clearly marked cycle lane.

2 Cross the bridge on the segregated **cycle path** and turn left along the riverside. Keep to the surfaced track known as **Barge Walk**.

MAP: OS Explorer 161 London South

START/FINISH: The Boaters Inn, Canbury Gardens, Kingston-upon-Thames; grid ref: TQ 179702

TRAILS/TRACKS: largely compacted gravel, with some surfaced sections

LANDSCAPE: riverside

PUBLIC TOILETS: Kingston-upon-Thames

TOURIST INFORMATION: Kingston-upon-Thames, tel 020 8547 5592

CYCLE HIRE: none available locally

THE PUB: The Boaters Inn, Kingston-upon-Thames

🛈 Give way to pedestrians on the shared riverside path

Getting to the start

From Seven Kings car park in Skerne Road go up Down Hall Road, alongside the railway, and head north to the Boaters Inn via the riverside path. The Boaters Inn is in Canbury Gardens, 0.5 mile (800m) north of Kingston Bridge on the eastern bank of the river. Lower Ham Road runs parallel to the A307 Richmond Road. There are pay-and-display car parks in Kingston-upon-Thames town centre.

Why do this cycle ride?

This is a straightforward ride suitable for all ages and links the pleasant market town of Kingston-upon-Thames with the familiar landmark of Hampton Court Palace via the excellent riverside path.

Researched and written by: James Hatts

3 Soon the watersports centre and yacht club of **Raven's Ait** (an island in the river) is reached. Remain on the riverside path.

4 **Thames Ditton Island**, with its 48 houses, is the next major landmark on the river. **The Pavilion**, designed by Sir Christopher Wren, is on the tow path here. When the surfaced track resumes you are

now on **Pavilion Terrace**. Follow the brick wall of Hampton Court Park; soon views of the Broad Walk will emerge. Closer to the palace the path gets wider and will be busy on a fine summer's day.

5 The ride ends at **Hampton Court Bridge**; you may wish to explore the Palace and grounds before returning to Kingston retracing your outward route.

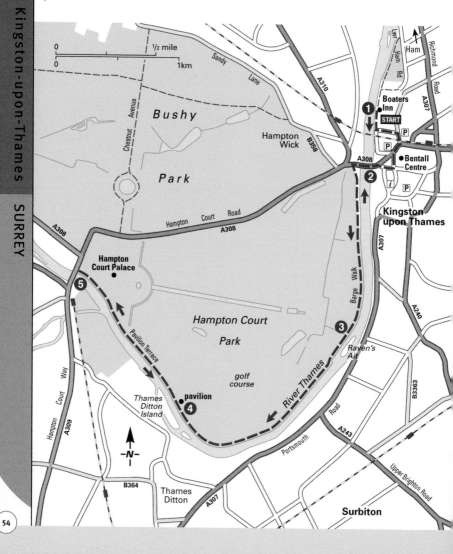

The Boaters Inn

The key to this modern pub's appeal lies in its splendid riverside location, with fine views of the busy Thames. There are moorings provided for those arriving by boat and the 10 per cent discount for rowers demonstrates that this waterside pub takes its river connections seriously. Colourful hanging baskets brighten the façade in summer, and the popular outdoor tables benefit from the shade of large trees in the adjacent Canbury Gardens. The Boaters is known locally for its live jazz and blues nights.

Food

Instead of conventional starters and main courses, the menu is divided into 'small plates' and 'big plates'. From the former you can order Cajun potato wedges and dip or deep-fried brie with fruit sauce; from the latter sausages with wholegrain mustard mash, and various fish, pasta and burger meals. Puddings include spotted dick and custard and blueberry cheesecake.

Family facilities

Children are welcome inside the bar. Facilities include a children's menu and baby-changing facilities.

Alternative refreshment stops

Choose from the pubs and cafés at Hampton Court.

☛ Where to go from here

Spend time exploring Henry VIII's magnificent Tudor palace at Hampton Court. Costumed and audio tours bring 500 years of history alive (www.hrp.org.uk). Visit Ham House, a fine Stuart house built in 1610 in beautiful gardens beside the

about the pub

The Boaters Inn
Canbury Gardens, Lower Ham Road
Kingston Upon Thames, Surrey
KT2 5AU
Tel: 020 8541 4672

DIRECTIONS: see Getting to the start; the pub is beside the Thames
PARKING: pay-and-display in Kingston town centre
OPEN: daily; all day
FOOD: daily; all day
BREWERY/COMPANY: free house
REAL ALE: Greene King IPA, Shepherd Neame Spitfire

Thames, containing an original collection of fine 17th-century furniture (www.nationaltrust.org.uk). Alternatively, stay local and discover more about the history of the town at the Kingston Museum (www.kingston.gov.uk/museums).

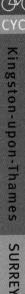

Along the Thames to the gardens at Kew

View the famous Royal Botanic Gardens at Kew from a surprisingly peaceful stretch of the Thames Path.

Kew

Kew – green fingers

Kew Gardens began life as a lawn for Kew Palace. The collection of exotic plants here was started in the 1740s. The in 1841, Queen Victoria handed the site to the nation as a public research institute. It is now the world's leading botanical research centre. Although this walk allows a glimpse along its boundaries, a visit inside is highly recommended, for which you should allow a few extra hours.

At Kew 200 horticultural staff are responsible for tending to the plants, including the tropical plants in the glasshouses and the Herbarium, where more than 6 million specimens of dried plants and fungi are stored. There are a further 100 scientists studying the medicinal importance of plants and many others based at one of the most visited parts of Kew, the Palm House.

Depending on the time of the year (May is best), you may be able to see part of the Rhododendron Dell from the Thames Path. The river provides these spectacular shrubs with the humidity they love. Rhododendrons are native to the Himalayas and were introduced to this country in the 1850s. There are now over 700 specimens of hardy species and hybrids in this Dell, some of which are unique to Kew Gardens.

Further along the Thames Path is the Syon Vista, an opening that affords views of the long, straight avenue leading to the Palm House. In keeping with the Victorian love of all things iron, the entire structure was built of iron and filled in with curved glass. The Palm House contains a tropical rainforest where plants are divided into three sections: African, American, and Asia and the Pacific. A central area displays the tallest palm trees.

the walk

1 From Earls Court direction, turn left out of the tube through the underpass and come out at a cul-de-sac of **shops**. Take either fork of the road and walk down to

The Pagoda in Kew Gardens

Sandycombe Road. Turn right along Sandycombe Road, which becomes Kew Gardens Road as it bends to the left. At Kew Road opposite the **Royal Botanic Gardens**, turn right and continue ahead to the traffic lights. Turn left and head towards Kew Green and St Anne's Church.

2 Take the path to the left of **St Anne's Church**, which was built for Queen Anne in 1714, and with your back to the church columns follow the main path to the right. Once across the green, continue along Ferry Lane which leads to the **Thames Path**.

3 Turn left here following the river along an attractive stretch of the path that borders **Kew Gardens** and offers the outsider a tempting view of the famous botanic gardens from the other side of a formidable ivy-clad walled ditch.

4 Just after a field, cross a ditch with metal gates to the left, signifying that this is the boundary of the **Old Deer Park**, which is now the home of the Royal Mid-Surrey Golf Course. Continue walking ahead for a further mile (1.6km) on the obvious track and cross **Richmond Lock** to reach the other side of the Thames.

5 Turn right and follow the **River Crane Walk** past a boatyard where the Capital Ring path veers away from the river to run by the Twickenham Campus of Brunel University. When you reach the road turn right and just past the convent, **Nazareth House**, turn right at a mini-roundabout, signposted 'Thames Path'.

Royal Botanical Gardens, Kew, in winter

3h00 — **7.5 MILES** — **12.1 KM** — **LEVEL 1 2 3**

MAP: OS Explorer 161 London South

START/FINISH: Kew Gardens tube; grid ref: TQ 192767

PATHS: mainly tow paths and tarmac

LANDSCAPE: riverside gardens and pubs

PUBLIC TOILETS: Syon House

TOURIST INFORMATION: Richmond, tel 020 8940 9125

THE PUB: The London Apprentice, Isleworth

🅛 Take care with children alongside the River Thames. The main road and Watermans Park is a somewhat run-down industrial area and so you may not want to do this section of the walk on your own. Keep to the canal route up to Kew Bridge.

Getting to the start

Kew Gardens tube station is on the District Line to Richmond. There's free parking on Kew Road (A307) after 10am every morning.

Researched and written by: Rebecca Harris, Deborah King

6 Turn left alongside the river towards the popular chalet-style Town Wharf pub and here, bear left and turn first right into **Church Street**. Beyond the square with The Old Blue School go over a bridge, past the riverside **London Apprentice pub**. After a church the road swings to the left along Park Road. Enter **Syon Park** and follow the tarmac road.

7 Exit the park keeping straight ahead, past the **garden centre** and along a walled path and turn right at the road. Cross a bridge and, if this path isn't flooded, turn right for a detour along the **Grand Union Canal**. Keep following the signs as the path will zig-zag back and forth from the main road. Otherwise continue along the road ahead, bearing right to go through **Watermans Park** and then rejoining the **Thames Path**.

what to look for

About 440yds (402m) past the ditch marking the boundary of the Old Deer Park, you'll come to a silver column showing the Meridian Line. The vista across to the King's Observatory includes the original Meridian Line that was used to set the King's time at the Houses of Parliament before 1884 when the Greenwich Meridian Line became the standard.

8 Past an ever-present row of houseboats, turn right to cross **Kew Bridge**. Cross the road at a pedestrian crossing, continue ahead and bear left into Mortlake Road. Turn right into Cumberland Road and left at the end to retrace your steps along **Kew Gardens Road** back to the tube station at the start of the walk.

The London Apprentice

WALK

Kew

SURREY

Taking its name from the apprentice lads of the various London livery companies who drank here, the pub dates back to Tudor times and enjoys an enviable position beside the Thames. It was patronised by Henry VIII and Oliver Cromwell, both of whom had close links with nearby Syon House, and was also a popular haunt of highwaymen, notably Dick Turpin; the underground tunnels linking the pub to the church were used by Thames smugglers. Although it has been modernised over the years you can still see an old mural panel in the low-beamed bar, 300-year-old plaster ceiling reliefs and a splendid Regency dining room. The pub is furnished with character and adorned with rugby memorabilia, and offers traditional pub food and excellent summer drinking on an attractive waterside terrace.

Food

Traditional menu choices range from sandwiches and old favourites like fish and chips and beef and Theakston pie, to Caesar salad, red Thai chicken curry and salmon with watercress sauce.

Family facilities

Families are welcome in the dining area until 9.30PM and there's a children's menu.

Alternative refreshment stops

The Kew Greenhouse, which was once the village bakery, has a quaint, refined atmosphere and serves steak pies, flans, quiches, Scotch beef and vegetarian dishes to a background of classical music. If it's a fine day, there are further riverside pubs, such as the Town Wharf halfway through the walk.

☞ Where to go from here

Make time to view the six glasshouses at Kew Gardens (www.kew.org). The beautiful Great Conservatory in Syon Park was built in 1820 for the 3rd Duke of Northumberland by the designer of Covent Garden Market, Charles Fowler. Syon House is still the Duke of Northumberland's London home and contains some of Robert Adam's finest interiors (www.syonpark.co.uk). Rugby-lovers will enjoy a behind-the-scenes look at the home of England rugby – Twickenham Stadium – and the history of the game with a visit to the Museum of Rugby and a tour of the stadium (www.rfu.com).

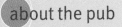

about the pub

The London Apprentice
62 Church Street, Isleworth
Middlesex TW7 6BG
Tel: 020 8560 1915
www.thespiritgroup.com

DIRECTIONS: adjacent to All Saint's Church and the River Thames in Isleworth (on walk just after point **6**)

PARKING: 20

OPEN: daily; all day

FOOD: daily; all day Friday, Saturday and Sunday

BREWERY/COMPANY: Spirit Group

REAL ALE: Courage Best, Fuller's London Pride, Wells Bombardier

DOGS: not allowed in the pub

The wetlands of Barnes

Barnes LONDON

Explore the award-winning London Wetland Centre and join the course of the Oxford and Cambridge Boat Race.

London Wetland Centre

Rowing boats, like birds, glide gracefully through water and also, like birds, you'll see plenty of them during this easy walk. Barnes has long been associated with the Oxford and Cambridge Boat Race. Indeed, the footbridge, added in 1895, was specifically designed to hold the crowds watching the last stage of the 4.33 mile (7km) race to Mortlake.

The riverside functions rather like a wildlife highway, providing a natural habitat for birds. There are plenty of them to see without having to put a foot inside the London Wetland Centre (LWC) – but to omit it would be to miss out on a very

rewarding experience. So why not extend the walk and visit the LWC? There are more than 2 miles (3.2km) of paths and 650yds (594m) of boardwalk to explore once you have paid the admission charge.

The Wildfowl and Wetlands Trust at Slimbridge in Gloucestershire was founded by Sir Peter Scott, son of the great explorer, Scott of the Antarctic. One of his father's diaries carries the words: 'teach the boy nature' and this was indeed achieved, for Peter Scott became a renowned painter and naturalist. In recognition of his achievements, a larger-than-life sculpture of him stands on a raised gravel island at the entrance to the LWC, the only inner city wetland reserve in the world. There are now nine wetland centres in the UK. This one began with four redundant reservoirs owned by Thames Water. They formed a partnership with the housing developer, Berkeley Homes, and donated £11 million

Left: London Wetlands Centre
Below: Hammersmith Bridge

to help construct the centre. The 105 acre (43ha) project took five years to complete.

Once inside, there are three main sections: world wetlands, reserve habitats and waterlife. The first contains captive birds from around the world – North America is accessed via a log cabin complete with authentic furniture. There are information panels too. One of them contradicts the popular belief that swans mate for life. Another tells us about meadowsweet, which is found in damp woods and marshes and used in herbal teas, mead flavouring and even air fresheners.

the walk

1 Turn left out of the London Wetland Centre and follow the path, initially to the left of the **Barnes Sports Centre** and then beside some sports fields. At a T-junction turn left along the well-signposted **Thames Path**, alongside the river in the direction of Hammersmith Bridge.

2 About 100yds (91m) along the path on the left is a **stone post**, denoting the 1-mile (1.6km) marker of the Oxford and Cambridge University Boat Race. Steve Fairbairn, who was born in 1862, founded the Head of the River Race and this was the start of the world-famous, annual boat race that traditionally takes place in March.

3 The landscaped area of smart flats on the left is called **Waterside** and, a few paces further, a red-brick building bears the name **Harrods Village**. Once past this, as if replicating the trademark Harrods colours

1h30 – **3.75 MILES** – **6 KM** – **LEVEL 1**23

MAP: OS Explorer 161 London South
START/FINISH: London Wetland Centre; grid ref: TQ 227767
PATHS: riverside tow path, muddy after rain
LANDSCAPE: views across Thames
PUBLIC TOILETS: at London Wetland Centre
TOURIST INFORMATION: Richmond, tel 020 8940 9125
THE PUB: The Bull's Head, Barnes, SW13

❶ Much of the route is alongside the River Thames, so take extra care with young children

Getting to the start

London Wetland Centre is off the A306 between Hammersmith Bridge and the A3003 in Barnes. There is a car park (free if visiting the Centre). Alternatively, you can access the walk (near Point 5) at Barnes Bridge railway station, or reach the Wetland Centre via bus 283 (known as 'the Duck Bus') from Hammersmith tube.

Researched and written by:
Rebecca Harris, Deborah King

of green and gold, is **Hammersmith Bridge**. Follow the path past **St Paul's School**, where *Planets* composer Gustav Holst was a music teacher. On the opposite side of the river, Chiswick Church's green roof is visible.

4 Continue along the riverside path to the end as it reaches **Barnes Bridge**.

5 Just past **The Bull's Head** pub by the bridge, turn left into Barnes High Street. At the next junction, by the little pond, bear left into Church Road. Past the **Sun Inn** is a row of village shops and 100yds (91m) further on, the lychgate to St Mary's Church. At the traffic lights continue ahead to return to the **London Wetland Centre** and the start of the walk.

what to look for

The development, Waterside, was constructed by Berkeley Homes after the company purchased 25 acres (10ha) and built the luxury homes that have a unique, bird's-eye view of the centre and its wildlife. Adjacent, the Harrods Village building was once used to store furniture by those taking up posts in the British Empire. Derelict, it was also sold to Berkeley Homes and it now contains 250 flats with green window frames. Even the security guard wears a Harrods green and gold uniform. At the rear of the Sun Inn is Barnes Bowling Club, where Sir Francis Drake is said to have taught Elizabeth I the game of bowls.

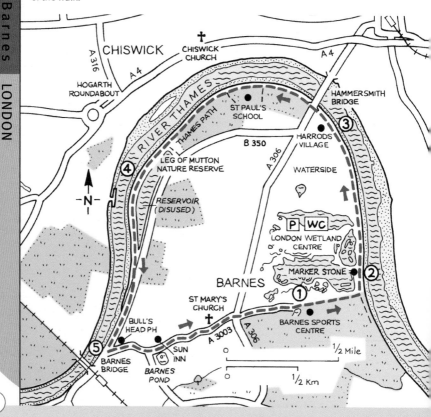

The Bull's Head

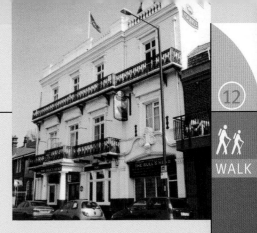

The imposing Bull's Head overlooking the Thames was established in 1684, and has made its reputation over the last 40 years as a top venue for mainstream, modern jazz and blues. Nightly concerts in the large back room draw music lovers from miles around, encouraged by some fine cask-conditioned ales from Young's, more than 200 wines (30 by the glass) and over 80 malt whiskies. The large, open-plan and bustling bar has a central island servery, plenty of cosy alcoves, a big fireplace stacked with bottles, and a lovely old mirror. The small rear patio is ideal for summer eating and drinking.

Food

Home-cooked meals such as soups, ciabatta sandwiches, roast of the day and steak and kidney pie are on offer in the bar, while fine Thai cooking from the Nuay Thai Bistro in the converted stable is available throughout the pub in the evening.

Family facilities

Children are very welcome in the pub during the day.

Alternative refreshment stops

Unlike many on-site cafés, the Water's Edge Café at the London Wetland Centre is a delight. It's bright and spacious, serves good-quality soups, sandwiches, salads and cakes, and has outdoor seating on large, wooden tables with umbrellas. The south-facing Sun Inn on Church Road, opposite Barnes duck pond, lives up to its name – it's quite a suntrap in summer.

☛ Where to go from here

A visit to the London Wetland Centre before or after your walk is a must (www.wwt.org.uk). Chiswick Church could once be reached by a ferry across the Thames, but since 1934 the only way is by bridge. The artist William Hogarth (from whom the Hogarth Roundabout takes its name) is buried in the churchyard. Also across the bridge is Chiswick House (www.english-heritage.org.uk), a fine English Palladian villa with a magnificent Blue Velvet Room and 18th-century classical gardens.

about the pub

The Bull's Head

373 Lonsdale Road
Barnes, London SW13 9PY
Tel: 020 8876 5241
www.thebullshead.com

DIRECTIONS: just before you turn left into Barnes High Road (on walk at Point **5**)	
PARKING: none	
OPEN: daily; all day	
FOOD: daily	
BREWERY/COMPANY: Young's Brewery	
REAL ALE: Young's Bitter, Special and Winter Warmer	
DOGS: welcome inside	

Barnes and Chiswick

A cross-river ride linking two London villages.

Chiswick House

Chiswick House is an attempt to re-create the kind of house and garden found in the suburbs of ancient Rome. It was designed in the 18th century by Richard Boyle, third Earl of Burlington, who employed William Kent to create sumptuous interiors to contrast with the pure white exterior. The historian Sir Kenneth Clark described the house as 'a masterpiece of domestic architecture'. The third Earl was a renowned patron of the arts, supporting writers including Alexander Pope and Jonathan Swift and the composer Handel. Surprisingly the villa was never intended as a residence but a temple of the arts. Two British prime ministers have died at the house, and it has played host to a huge number of international royals and statesmen. The Earl paid great attention

A double staircase and two-storey portico decorate the front of Chiswick House

1h30 — **4 MILES** — **6.4 KM** — **LEVEL 1 2 3**

MAP: OS Explorer 161 London South

START/FINISH: The Coach and Horses, Barnes High Street; grid ref: TQ 216764

TRAILS/TRACKS: nearly all surfaced tracks and roads

LANDSCAPE: riverside, parkland and streets

PUBLIC TOILETS: none on route

TOURIST INFORMATION: Hounslow, tel 0845 456 2929

CYCLE HIRE: none available locally

THE PUB: Coach and Horses, Barnes, SW13

🅘 You will need to carry your bike up some stairs to cross a bridge

Getting to the start

Barnes is close to the A205 South Circular Road. The Coach and Horses is in Barnes High Street, close to the river. There is on-street pay-and-display parking in the area.

Why do this cycle ride?

This is a short circular ride linking the London villages of Barnes and Chiswick, taking in the breathtaking Chiswick House and its grounds, as well as offering vistas of the Thames.

Researched and written by: James Hatts

to the grounds, whose features include an obelisk, temple, amphitheatre, cascade and wilderness.

the ride

1 Turn left out of the pub and approach the river. Bear left along the river until you reach **Barnes Bridge station**.

A closer view of Chiswick House

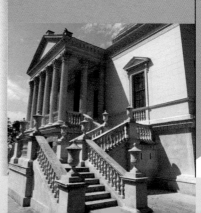

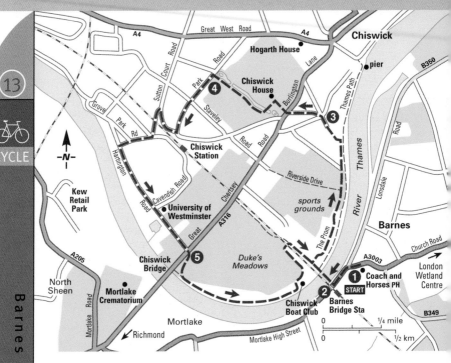

Take the stairs here to cross **Barnes Bridge**. On the far side of the bridge descend the steps. Do not follow the riverside path; turn left and head inland a short distance to reach a wider, surfaced track. Turn right here along **The Promenade** and pass the bandstand and other sports ground amenities. Where **Riverside Drive** turns sharply inland, continue straight ahead by the river. Notice the unusual sculptures here. When **Chiswick Pier** is in sight and you reach the cycling prohibited signs, bear inland up the long lane to the roundabout.

At the roundabout bear left towards the off-licence and take the right-hand fork along Grantham Road. Cross Burlington Lane to enter **Chiswick House Grounds**. Observe any signs restricting cycling in this area. Head straight on towards the entrance to **Chiswick House**. By the gates, turn left to cross the bridge by the **cascades**. Turn right

up the side of the lake and exit the grounds on to **Park Road**.

Turn left along Park Road and keep straight ahead at Staveley Road. On reaching **Chiswick Station**, turn right along Sutton Court Road. Take a sharp left turn to cross the railway on **Grove Park Bridge**. Take the second right along Grove Park Road. At Hartington Road turn left, then beyond Cavendish Road, the **University of Westminster**'s sport ground looms on the left.

Cross **Great Chertsey Road** (the approach to Chiswick Bridge) and pick up the lane on the other side that loops round towards the river and skirts **Duke's Meadow**. The track eventually wiggles inland around Chiswick Boat Club. Soon the track dives under the **railway**; turn right here and return to Barnes Bridge. Cross the bridge and return to the south bank of the Thames.

The Coach and Horses

First leased by Young's Brewery in 1831, this fine old coaching inn retains plenty of character and its unassuming frontage doesn't betray what lies behind it. A narrow archway leads to a long beer garden, with a boules pitch and small play area at the very rear. Behind the stained glass lies a small, cosy bar filled with a cast of regulars who create a friendly, welcoming atmosphere. Furnishings are traditional and décor includes St George's flags draped around the bar, photographs of Barnes in days gone by lining the walls, and a selection books to peruse while enjoying a pint of Young's Special.

about the pub

Coach and Horses
27 Barnes High Street, Barnes
London SW13 9LW
Tel: 020 8876 2695

DIRECTIONS: on the south side of Barnes High Street, between the village centre and the river	
PARKING: on-street pay and display	
OPEN: daily; all day	
FOOD: daily; all day	
BREWERY/COMPANY: Young's Brewery	
REAL ALE: Young's Bitter, Special and seasonal beers	

Food

A barbecue counter in the garden serves traditional fare such as sausages and burgers throughout the summer. A more conventional menu is also available, with the usual hot dishes and a range of ploughman's meals.

Family facilities

Children are welcome inside. There's a family dining room if the weather is inclement, while on sunny days children can enjoy the play area in the garden.

Alternative refreshment stops

There are various pubs and cafés in Barnes and Chiswick.

☛ Where to go from here

Just along the road is the unique, state-of-the-art Wildfowl and Wetlands Trust Centre, set in 105 acres (42.5ha) of wild wetlands. Here you can explore lakes and marshes, view birds and animals from multistorey hides and learn more about wildlife at the interactive Discovery Centre (www.wetlandcentre.org.uk). Don't miss out on a visit to Chiswick House along the route (www.english-heritage.org.uk). In Chiswick, just off the A4 in Hogarth Lane, you can visit Hogarth House, once home to the artist William Hogarth (1697–1764), to view displays on the artist's life and many of his satirical engravings.

From Fulham to Hammersmith

Discover Harrods furniture repository, Fulham football club and a bishop's palace.

Fulham

Fulham Football Club has played at the riverside Craven Cottage ground since 1896. Now with a capacity of 22,200, it continues to play an important part in English football. The team known as 'the Cottagers' returned home for the 2004 season after a couple of years ground-sharing with Queen's Park Rangers. The building, which lends its name to the ground, is a listed structure and can be seen clearly from the cycle route.

Fulham Palace was a residence of the Bishop of London for more than 1,200 years between 704 and 1973, and once boasted the longest moat in England. In its current form it comprises a fascinating mixture of architectural styles, from the red brick of the Tudor courtyard to the elegant Georgian east frontage. Excavations have revealed evidence of neolithic

Fulham Palace the residence of the Bishops of London until 1973

Fulham football ground, Craven Cottage

and Roman settlements on the site. The palace gardens achieved fame in the 17th century when rare species such as the magnolia were imported and grown here for the first time. Today a museum is based In the early 19th-century part of the palace where you can find out about the Palace's history.

the ride

1 Ride upstream from Putney Bridge along **Putney Embankment**. Look out for the 'UBR' bollard marking the start of the annual University Boat Race. Continue past the various boathouses and clubhouses. Towards the end of the surfaced section is **Leader's Gardens**, to the left.

2 The path becomes rough (and muddy at times) beyond the bridge that carries the tow path over **Beverley Brook**. Continue past the Sea Scout headquarters. Barn Elms school sports centre is through the trees to your left and across the river there are views of **Craven Cottage**. Ignore the National Cycle Network route signed to the left and remain on the tow path to Harrods Village and **Hammersmith Bridge**.

3 Pass underneath the bridge and use the ramp on the far side to reach the road level. Cross the river here and take the first right into Worlidge Street. Turn right into Queen Caroline Street to return towards the river and the **Riverside Studios**. After a left turn into Crisp Road, bear left into Chancellor's Road. Take the first right into Distillery Road. Bear right into Winslow Road, and take a left into **Manbre Road**.

1h30 | **4.5 MILES** | **7.2 KM** | **LEVEL 1 2 3**

MAP: OS Explorer 161 London South
START/FINISH: Putney Embankment; grid ref: TQ 240757
TRAILS/TRACKS: unsurfaced tracks, surburban streets
LANDSCAPE: riverside and parkland
PUBLIC TOILETS: in Bishop's Park
TOURIST INFORMATION: Richmond, tel 020 8940 9125
CYCLE HIRE: London Recumbents, Battersea Park, tel 020 7498 6543
THE PUB: The Coat and Badge, 8 Lacy Road
⓵ Some short, steep climbs and a couple of longer ascents through woodland

Getting to the start

Putney Embankment is to the west of Putney Bridge on the southern bank of the river. If parking at the Putney Exchange car park, turn left into Putney High Street then left at the Lower Richmond Road to reach the start point. Putney is just inside the South Circular Road.

Why do this cycle ride?

This is an easy circuit with lots to see, from the former Harrods Furniture Depository to Fulham Football Club's famous Craven Cottage ground, as well as Fulham Palace, once the residence of the Bishop of London.

Researched and written by: James Hatts

14

CYCLE

Fulham LONDON

4 Use the **cyclists-only link** between Manbre Road and Rannoch Road. At Crabtree Lane turn right, then bear left into Woodlawn Road.

5 **Queensmill School** is the next landmark to spot; beyond the school take a right into Queensmill Road to get closer to the river; continue along Stevenage Road until you reach **Craven Cottage**.

6 Beyond the football ground enter into **Bishop's Park** on the right-hand side and follow the signed cycle route past **Fulham Palace**. Leave the park through the gate by All Saints Church and ride up the slope to reach **Putney Bridge Approach**. Turn right to cross the bridge and return to the start.

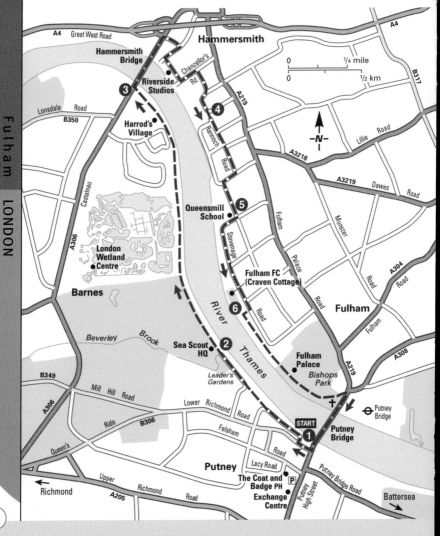

The Coat and Badge

Tucked away in a quiet street, yet just a stone's throw from the bustle of Putney High Street, this light and spacious pub-restaurant offers a civilised retreat from the crowds. The L-shaped room is filled with an eclectic mix of old tables, chairs and relaxing leather settees, bookshelves scattered with books, vases and plants, and warm, yellow-painted walls covered with paintings and objets d'art. The pub has a rowing theme, including a river mural of two rowers, a set of oars and the impressive list of the winners of The Coat & Badge Sculling Race. On warm summer days head for the leafy courtyard garden; in winter relax with a drink in front of the open fire.

Food

The imaginative menu changes monthly and features starters such as smoked haddock cakes with spicy chilli sauce or Caesar salad, followed by Cumberland sausages with parsley mash, fresh pasta and salads, or chargrilled rib-eye steak. There are also daily specials, lunchtime sandwiches and summer barbecues.

Family facilities
Children are welcome before 7PM.

Alternative refreshment stops
You will find a good choice of pubs and cafés in Putney town centre.

☛ Where to go from here
Don't miss the views across the lakes and marshes of the London Wetland Centre on this ride. Why not return and explore it on foot, visit a hide and the informative and interactive Discovery Centre to learn more about the wildlife living here and so close to central London (www.wetlandcentre.org.uk).

about the pub

The Coat and Badge
8 Lacy Road, Putney
London SW15 1NL
Tel: 020 8788 4900
www.geronimo-inns.co.uk

DIRECTIONS: see Getting to the start; the pub is opposite the car park

PARKING: at the Exchange Centre, directly opposite the pub

OPEN: daily; all day

FOOD: daily

BREWERY/COMPANY: Geronimo Inns

REAL ALE: Young's

Wimbledon Common and beyond

Discover some of south west London's hidden villages.

Wimbledon Windmill

A popular local landmark, the Windmill was built in 1817 to serve local residents who didn't trust the 'factory produced' flour from the large mills on the River Wandle. The mill's working life ended in 1864 when Earl Spencer, the lord of the manor, announced his intention to enclose Wimbledon Common and build a new manor house on the site of the mill. Local opposition led to a six-year legal battle, resolved by the 1871 Wimbledon and Putney Commons Act, which handed over the common to the local community. The mill was then converted into homes for six families. Robert Baden-Powell, founder of the Scout movement, lived at the adjacent Mill House for a time

and wrote part of *Scouting for Boys* here. A museum opened in the Windmill in 1975; more recently Lottery funding has enabled the sails to be restored to working order. The museum tells the story of windmills around the world, including early Persian and Greek examples, as well as modern wind farms. An information centre with general information on Wimbledon and Putney Commons is a short distance from the Windmill.

the ride

1 From Southside Common take the short cycle lane north along **The Green**, which almost immediately turns on to the common, with **Rushmere Pond** to the left. Soon the gravel path crosses Cannizaro Road before converging at the junction between West Side Common and The Causeway. Turn left here along **Camp Road**,

Left: Wimbledon Common
Below: Wimbledon Windmill

with the **Fox & Grapes** pub to your right. At Camp View, take Sunset Road through the gate signed for **Thatched Cottage**. Close to Springwell Cottage, look for the **gate** to the left, marked for cyclists. Take this path; this section is unsurfaced and involves bouncing over many exposed tree roots. Much of it is also shared with horse riders, so the path can be churned up.

2 When you reach a bridge over **Beverley Brook**, remain on the east bank and turn right. Past the playing fields, turn left across the bridge and head for the footbridge over the main road. Use the toucan crossings here to reach the Robin Hood Gate into **Richmond Park**.

3 Go straight ahead along the park road, then bear right on reaching the car park. There are views across **Pen Ponds** to your left. Here the path is wide and well surfaced. There is a climb up to **White Lodge**, home of the Royal Ballet School. To the left there is a great view along Queen's Ride. The path swoops downhill to the T-junction with Sawyer's Hill; turn right here and join the traffic-free **cycle path** parallel to the road.

4 Leave the park at **Roehampton Gate**, taking the right-hand fork along Prior Lane and the first right into **Danebury Avenue**. There is no through route for motor vehicles, but there is a gap between the bollards for cyclists. Continue past the bus terminus and follow the avenue as it curves round to meet Roehampton Lane. Cross over here and go straight ahead along

1h30 — **7.5 MILES** — **12.1 KM** — **LEVEL 1 2 3**

CYCLE

Wimbledon LONDON

MAP: OS Explorer 161 London South

START/FINISH: Southside Common, Wimbledon Village; grid ref: TQ 237710

TRAILS/TRACKS: mixed; some well-surfaced paths, some rough tracks

LANDSCAPE: woodland, parkland and suburban streets

PUBLIC TOILETS: at gates of Richmond Park

TOURIST INFORMATION: Richmond, tel 020 8940 9125

CYCLE HIRE: Smith Brothers, 14 Church Road, Wimbledon, tel 020 8946 2270

THE PUB: Fox & Grapes, Wimbledon Common, SW19

🛑 Some rough unsurfaced sections; may be muddy after heavy rain

Getting to to the start

Southside Common is just off Wimbledon High Street in Wimbledon Village. There is metered parking around Southside Common.

Why do this cycle ride?

This circuit links three of south-west London's often under-appreciated green spaces: Wimbledon Common, Putney Heath and Richmond Park. There is a marked contrast between the more natural, rural feel to Wimbledon Common and Richmond's carefully managed royal park.

Researched and written by: James Hatts

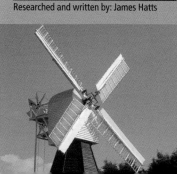

Roehampton High Street. Turn right into Medfield Street and pick up the **cycle path** on to Putney Heath by the war memorial. Beyond **Scio Pond** the path comes close to the A306 before passing underneath the A3 via a subway.

5 Beyond the subway take the right-hand fork (Windmill Road). At the green gate turn right for access to the **windmill**, museum, information centre and tea room.

6 From the windmill go straight ahead through the **green gate**, but keep a good lookout for the left-hand fork. Take this path, which crosses over two horse rides. Soon the path emerges on to the road at **West Place**, with its picturesque cottages. Take a right turn into Camp Road for the pub or continue straight on to return to **Southside Common** along the outward route.

Fox & Grapes

The Fox & Grapes, which dates back to 1787, looks and feels like a small rural pub, set as it is on the edge of Wimbledon Common. The main bar with its high-beamed ceiling once housed stables in the 18th century, while the original bar to the left is now a smoke-free area with cosy stools and benches. One of the pub's claims to fame is that from 1868 it was used for 20 years as the changing rooms for what later became Wimbledon Football Club. The landlord's enthusiasm for fine wines is reflected in the extensive wine list; ale drinkers will not be disappointed with the Bombardier bitter on tap.

Food

An appetising tapas menu with ingredients sourced from Spain is available all day. You could also try the pub's speciality pork pies, served as a ploughman's lunch and made to a 19th-century recipe, using Gloucester old spot pork.

Family facilities

Children are made very welcome throughout the pub.

Alternative refreshment stops

Try the tea room at Wimbledon Windmill or one of the pubs around Wimbledon Common, including the Crooked Billet and the Hand-in-Hand.

☞ Where to go from here

At the Wimbledon Lawn Tennis Museum (www.wimbledon.org), pictures, displays and memorabilia trace the development of the game over the last century. See the world-famous Championship's trophies,

about the pub

Fox & Grapes
9 Camp Road, Wimbledon Common
London SW19
Tel: 020 8946 5599

DIRECTIONS: Camp Road can be reached via The Causeway from Wimbledon High Street (A219)

PARKING: on-road metered parking around Southside Common and The Causeway

OPEN: daily; all day

FOOD: daily; all day

BREWERY/COMPANY: free house

REAL ALE: Wells Bombardier

as well as archive film and video footage of great players in action, and enjoy a behind-the-scenes guided tour of Centre Court, No 1 Court and the press interview room.

CYCLE

Wimbledon LONDON

Hampstead Heath

Explore one of London's best-loved open spaces, a one-time spa and the scene of an unfortunate murder in the 1950s.

Hampstead Heath

A walk on the sprawling Heath, just 4 miles (6.4km) from central London, is the perfect escape from the pressures of city life. Hampstead first became fashionable in the 18th century when the discovery of spring water transformed the village into a Georgian spa town. There was no stopping the writers, poets and painters who were attracted by the green, open spaces and healthy aspect. This remains the case today, although the only spring water you'll find now is that produced by the large manufacturers and sold by the bottle in shops and pubs.

Hampstead has another claim to fame or, perhaps in this case, notoriety. The village was the scene of a murder that signalled the end of capital punishment in this country. The crime was committed by Ruth Ellis, who became the last woman to be hanged in Britain. Ruth Ellis was a Soho nightclub hostess. Racing driver, David Blakely ended their relationship and as he left the Magdala Tavern in South Hill Park road (near the end of the walk), she shot him – he was dead on arrival at hospital. Ellis remained adamant that she intended to kill Blakely. The jury took less than 30 minutes to agree on a verdict, and the rest is history.

Apart from that episode, Hampstead remains pretty much untainted by modern life. There are plenty of opportunities for

you to wander off in to the wilder side of the Heath should you wish. Indeed, one of the delights here is in exploring the many pathways that criss-cross the grasslands and delve into woodland.

Covering almost 800 acres (324ha), the Heath contains 25 ponds and a mixture of ancient woodland, bogs, hedgerows and grassland. Many writers seeking inspiration have discovered that this environment is the perfect antidote to writers' block. In fact, Keats had one of his most creative periods after moving to Hampstead.

the walk

1 Turn left outside Hampstead tube down Hampstead High Street and left into **Flask Walk**. Go down the hill past the old Wells and Campden Wash House (1888) and **Burgh House**, both on the left. Follow Well Walk, past the Wells Tavern on the right until it reaches East Heath Road. Cross over and continue along the path opposite.

2 Follow the tree-lined path for 200yds (183m), as far as a junction and a **water tap**. Continue for a further 100yds (91m) and turn left at the first **bench** on the right. The track continues before coming to a gate to the left indicating the entrance to the 112 acres (45ha) of **Kenwood House**.

3 In front of you two oak trees are surrounded by logs, with four paths fanning out. Take the path at 1 o'clock position, bearing off to the left as you walk around the trees. The path descends gently, passing some benches with views over to Highgate village. Continue ahead into woodland. If you have a dog, it should be

Kenwood House

2h00 — **4.25 MILES** **6.8 KM** — **LEVEL 123**

16

WALK

Hampstead Heath

LONDON

on a lead now. Carry straight on through a wooden gate along an ivy-lined path, passing two **cottages**, then bear right towards **Kenwood House car park**.

4 Bear right through the car park, following signs to Kenwood House. Turn right, through the main gates. Take the path on the right of the house, through a low ivy arch and on to a wide terrace that overlooks the grounds. Beyond the **tea room** take a left fork through Stable Field to a **pergola**, for fine views including the Gerkin, St Paul's, the Millennium Wheel and the Post Office Tower. Next, take a path to the right, passing a metal gate.

5 Turn left, downhill, passing to the left of a **lake**. Keep ahead through some

A sunny-day stroll along Hampstead Heath's well-trodden trails

MAP: OS Explorer 173 London North
START/FINISH: Hampstead tube; grid ref: TQ 264858
PATHS: mainly well-trodden heathland tracks
LANDSCAPE: heath and woodland scenery and some impressive views across London
PUBLIC TOILETS: Highgate
TOURIST INFORMATION: Camden, tel 020 7974 5974
THE PUB: The Flask, Highgate, N6

Getting to the start

Hampstead lies on the A502 north west of Camden. Parking is beside the heath off East Heath Road. It's best accessed using the Underground's Northern Line, via Euston and Camden Town.

Researched and written by:
Rebecca Harris, Deborah King

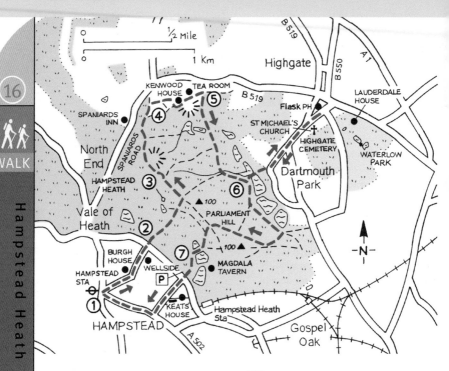

woodland and go through a metal barrier. Continue along the track ahead, take the right fork (a road – **Millfield Lane** is visible ahead) and head uphill. (For **The Flask** pub, don't take the right fork, instead, walk up Millfield Lane and turn left up Merton Road until it joins a main road – **High Gate West Hill**. Turn left here and continue up hill. The Flask is at the fork ahead – with Highgate West Hill continuing to the left and South Grove to the right. Return back down Millfield Lane.) At a fork take the right-hand path, which then descends. Follow the tarmac path taking the left fork past a **pond**.

6 Pass **three more ponds**, turning sharp right after the last one, along a path that climbs uphill. At the next junction follow the right-hand path to the top of **Parliament Hill**. Continue straight ahead down this path, through the trees and between two ponds. Head uphill for 50yds (46m).

7 At the fork bear right through **West Field Gate**. The winding paths open out on to heath. Follow the tarmac path and where the paths cross turn right into East Heath Road. Cross over into **Downshire Hill** and turn second left into Keats Grove to visit **Keats House**. Otherwise continue along Downshire Hill, turning right at the end into **Rosslyn Hill**, then back up to Hampstead tube.

what to look for

Built in 1703, Burgh House was the home of Dr William Gibbons, who first highlighted the medicinal qualities of Hampstead's spa water. Just past this, notice the plaque on Wellside, a residential house built on the site of the original pump house. The painter, John Constable, lived at 40 Well Walk for ten years. He is buried in the nearby St John's churchyard.

The Flask

Dating back to 1663, this characterful pub was built as the last watering hole before London and takes its name from the flasks, which were obtained from the premises and filled with the chalybeate spa water from Hampstead Wells. Dick Turpin hid from his pursuers in the cellars, and T S Elliot and Sir John Betjeman enjoyed a glass or two of ale here. Parts of the rambling interior are listed and include the original bar with sash windows that lift up at opening time. The two original low-beamed and panelled bars (the Committee Room and Snug Bar) have flagstone floors, with further split-level rooms featuring wooden floors and an eclectic mix of tastefully modern furnishings filling cosy corners and alcoves. There's a lovely enclosed area at the front with tables and chairs, baskets of flowers and wisteria over the original pale brick walls.

about the pub

The Flask
77 Highgate West Hill
Highgate, London N6 3BU
Tel: 020 8348 7346
www.theflaskhighgate.co.uk

DIRECTIONS: nearest tube: Archway or Highgate	
PARKING: none	
OPEN: daily; all day	
FOOD: daily; all day Saturday	
BREWERY/COMPANY: Mitchells & Butlers	
REAL ALE: six changing guest beers	
DOGS: welcome inside	

Food

The blackboard menu changes twice daily. Choices range from sandwiches and platters to main courses such as crayfish linguine, hand-made sausages with mash and onion gravy, and seared ginger duck with sweet potato and wilted baby spinach.

Family facilities

Children of all ages are welcome. Expect half-portions of adult dishes and high chairs, and baby food/bottles will be warmed for you.

Alternative refreshment stops

The café at Kenwood House, with its outdoor herb garden and sun canopies, is a pleasant place for lunch or a lighter snack. Just off the route is the Spaniards Inn, once a toll booth with snug, oak-panelled rooms with open fires and low ceilings.

☛ Where to go from here

Keats House is a Grade I-listed building. John Keats wrote Ode to a Nightingale here, apparently after hearing one sing in the gardens of the Spaniards Inn. Many of his personal possessions are also on display. Kenwood House in Hampstead Lane is an outstanding neo-classical house containing one of the most important collections of paintings given to the nation. Sumptuous rooms contain works by Rembrandt, Turner, Gainsborough and Reynolds (www.english-heritage.org.uk).

Along the River Wandle

Discover one of London's forgotten rivers.

Merton and Morton

Merton Priory was an Augustinian house founded on the site where the Roman road from London to Chichester crosses the River Wandle. Among those educated at the priory were Thomas Becket and the only English pope to date, Nicholas Brakespeare. A church the size of Westminster Abbey once stood on the site now occupied by Sainsbury's Savacentre. After the Reformation the site of the priory became known as Merton Abbey. From the 1660s it became a textile manufacturing centre, and most famously William Morris's calico works were here at Merton Abbey. The Regent Street store Liberty had its printworks here between 1904 and 1972. Several of the buildings are still standing, including the wheel house and water wheel that drove the rinsing spools. The water wheel is still operational and now drives a potters' wheel. Much of the site is occupied by a craft market and farmer's market. The complex is busiest at weekends, but there is plenty to see during the week too.

The estate of Morden Hall Park was created by the Hatfeild family who made their money from snuff milling on the Wandle. Gilliat Hatfeild left the park to the National Trust on his death in 1941. A well-liked philanthropist, Gilliat lived in Morden Cottage rather than the Hall because he considered it better suited to a bachelor. The walled Kitchen Garden, that once required 14 gardeners to maintain it, now houses the car park, garden centre and tea room. Outbuildings such as the tool shed

and boiler house have been converted into workshops for independent craftsmen and women. The National Trust has restored Hatfeild's fine 1922 rose garden, which contains over 2,000 roses.

the ride

1 From The Ship follow the **London Cycle Network** sign for Wandsworth south along Jew's Row past the bus garage. Although cyclists are provided for in the gyratory system, families with small children will prefer to dismount and use the pedestrian crossing to reach old York Road. Pass under the railway bridge at **Wandsworth Town Station** and continue until the traffic lights. Here there is a toucan crossing for pedestrians and cyclists on the right-hand side. Cross over on to Armoury Way and continue until you reach another toucan crossing. Cross here and follow Ram Street, with the **Young's Ram Brewery** on your right.

2 With the **Southside shopping centre** on your right, proceed down Garratt Lane. This is probably the most difficult section of the ride, so you may prefer to push your bike. At Mapleton Road use the toucan crossing, then turn right across the bridge. At the park gates turn sharp left on to the signed cycle trail. The 55-acre (22ha) **King George's Park** was opened by George V in 1923. Spot the unusual blue plaque just before the crossing at Kimber Road. The path now runs between the river and the **adventure playground**. Part of the route is known as Foster's Way, named after Corporal Edward Foster of the 13th Battalion (Wandsworth) of the East Surrey Regiment, who was awarded the Victoria Cross in 1917.

Morden Hall Park

3h00 | **11 MILES** | **17.7 KM** | **LEVEL 123**

CYCLE

Wandsworth LONDON

3 Leave the park extension through the gates and continue straight ahead along **Acuba Road**. Beware of the confusing cycle route signage here. At Ravensbury Road turn left. Once you have joined Ravensbury Terrace, turn right into Penwith Road and cross the river. At the traffic lights turn right. Again, it is wise to dismount for this section. Once you have passed Earlsfield station turn right into **Summerley Street** at Barclays Bank. When you reach Trewint Street turn right and cross the river, then join the riverside path to the left. At a fork – take the unsurfaced track to the left.

4 At Plough Lane there is a toucan crossing. It is necessary to cross the river as well as the road at this point; the path moves to the east bank. Look out for the metal **Wandle Trail mile marker** on the left. The path is once again well-surfaced and is on a tree-lined embankment high above the water, shaded in summer. Once you have gone under the railway bridge continue straight on with the **Wandle Meadow Nature Park** on your right. The path soon exits on to a concrete road.

5 At North Road turn right, then left at the mini roundabout on to East Road. Once again the signs disappear, so don't miss the right turn at **All Saints Road**. Take a left at Hanover Road and again at Leyton Road. Go past the fire brigade gate and turn left. Use the toucan crossing at Merton High Street. Before the footbridge leading to Savacentre turn right along the riverside path. At the next bridge veer right and head for the small stone arch leading to another toucan crossing at Merantun Way. Cross the road to **Merton Abbey Mills**.

MAP: OS Explorer 161 London South

START/FINISH: The Ship, Jew's Row, Wandsworth, grid ref: TQ 259754 or the Southside Centre car park in Wandsworth

TRAILS/TRACKS: largely tarmac paths with some suburban roads and compacted gravel

LANDSCAPE: parkland and waterside

PUBLIC TOILETS: at Morden Hall Park

TOURIST INFORMATION: Merton, tel 020 8946 9192

CYCLE HIRE: London Recumbents in Battersea Park, tel 020 7498 6543

THE PUB: The Ship, Wandsworth, SW18

❗ The section between The Ship and King George's Park involves riding on some busy roads

Getting to the start

The Ship and Jew's Row is just off the Wandsworth Gyratory System, south of Wandsworth Bridge. There is on-street metered parking (maximum 4 hours) on Jew's Row. Alternatively, park at the Southside Centre multistorey car park on Garrett Lane in Wandsworth (on the route at Point **2**).

Why do this cycle ride?

This is an enjoyable ride linking the Thames with the beautiful rose gardens of Morden Hall Park, via the industrial heritage of Merton Abbey Mills.

Researched and written by: James Hatts

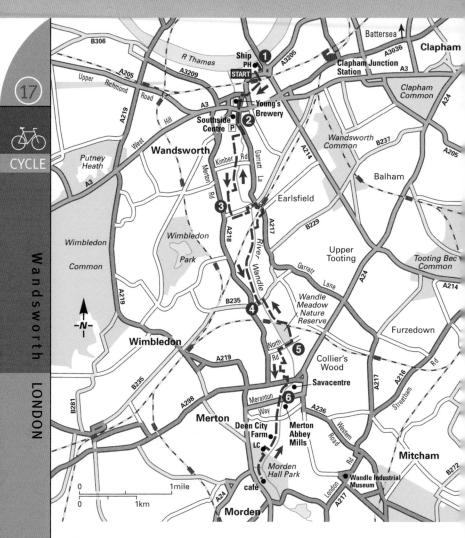

6 Continue past Merton Abbey Mills. At the road bridge cross Windsor Avenue. Here the riverside path doubles as the driveway of **Deen City Farm**. On reaching the farm gate keep straight on past the National Trust sign into **Morden Hall Park**. Turn left at the T-junction to reach a level crossing with the Wimbledon branch of Croydon Tramlink. Soon after the crossing, turn left away from the tramline through the unpromising gap in the fence. This section runs through the

Morden Hall Park Wetlands. A National Trust panel explains the wildlife you are likely to spot. At the next junction turn left and cross two bridges in quick succession. At the larger iron bridge turn right for the National Trust shop and café in the **walled garden** or just explore the park and rose gardens before tackling the return journey.

The Ship

The Ship, next to Wandsworth Bridge on the Thames, exudes a lively, bustling atmosphere. From the road, this 19th-century building has nothing to distinguish it from any other pub, apart from the figurehead above an unused doorway. However, if you approach the pub from the river walk, you will pass through a two-level terrace with a barbecue area and lots of seating, summer bar and colourful trellises and flower boxes, to the attractive, light and airy, conservatory-style lounge bar. Here you will find heavy oak tables and chairs, old desks and even a butcher's table, and there's a central wood-burning stove and an open-to-view kitchen area.

Food
The emphasis of the imaginative menu is on free-range produce from the landlord's organic farm. Expect the likes of rack of lamb with rosemary and ratatouille, handmade sausages, shepherd's pie, home-made leek and rocket soup and poached haddock with parsley mash.

Family facilities
Children are very welcome inside the pub. High chairs and smaller portions are available.

Alternative refreshment stops
There is the William Morris at Merton Abbey Mills and the National Trust Riverside Café at Morden Hall Park.

☛ Where to go from here
On Wandsworth High Street you will find Young's Ram Brewery. Beer has been brewed continuously alongside the River Wandle since 1581 and the present brewery was founded in 1675. You can learn more about the history of Young's and the brewing process at the Visitor Centre, where tours of the brewery (over 14s only) and the stables (over 5s) can be arranged (www.youngs.co.uk). Children will enjoy a visit to Deen City Farm at Merton Abbey, a fascinating community farm where they can learn how to look after animals and plants (www.deencityfarm.co.uk). Secrets of the powerful River Wandle and its industrial past can be explored at the Wandle Industrial Museum in Mitcham (www.wandle.org.uk). For more information about Merton Abbey Mills contact www.mertonabbeymills.com, and for Morden Hall Park www.nationaltrust.org.uk.

about the pub

The Ship
41 Jew's Row, Wandsworth
London SW18 1TB
Tel: 020 8870 9667
www.theship.co.uk

DIRECTIONS: see Getting to the start

PARKING: on-street parking in Jew's Row limited to 4 hours on weekdays

OPEN: daily; all day

FOOD: daily; all day

BREWERY/COMPANY: Young's Brewery

REAL ALE: Young's Bitter, Special, Triple A and Waggle Dance

Around Holland Park

Holland Park has something for everyone: cinemas, cafés, wildlife and memorable architecture.

Films and Architectural Delights

The walk begins at Notting Hill Gate, for it wouldn't be fair to mention 'diversions' without including Holland Park's lively neighbour, Notting Hill. Most cinema audiences throughout the world are now familiar with this area thanks to the film of the same name. And of course, there's that colourful annual event known as the Notting Hill Carnival that takes place in August, plus the world-famous Portobello Road antiques market, but where does Holland Park fit into all this?

Holland Park may lack the racy pace of its neighbour but it s comfortable in its own, refined skin. Some of the architecture here is truly memorable. The area includes some of the most sought-after properties in London, but it has a soft centre in the form of a delightful park, in which lie the partial ruins of a Jacobean mansion, Holland House. Lady Holland hosted some lavish parties here. The building was largely destroyed during the Blitz in World War Two. The section that remains is now a youth hostel. For less than the cost of a theatre ticket you can stay overnight in one of the loveliest parks in London. You can still see some remnants from the house's glorious past, such as the old ballroom (which is now a Marco Pierre White restaurant called The Belvedere) and the manicured garden.

And that's not all. Take the striking Gate Cinema, for example: it was was once a theatre and now shows international films. If it's open take a peek inside, as you should with the Coronet, a little further on.

The Coronet is the only cinema in London to permit smoking during the film, although smokers are restricted to the dress circle. Addison Road also has its fair share of architectural delights. Keep an eye out for No 8, a monster of a house that was designed for the store magnate, Sir Ernest Debenham.

the walk

1 From Notting Hill Gate tube head towards Holland Park Avenue, passing the **Gate Cinema** and a few paces further, the Coronet. This busy road is lined with some quaint shops and pubs, including one of the finest organic butchers in London. (To reach **The Ladbroke Arms**, turn right before Holland Park tube along Ladbroke Grove, then first left along Ladbroke Road.)

2 About 650yds (594m) after Holland Park tube turn left into **Holland Park Gardens**. Just after the red-brick school on the right the road joins Addison Road. Carry on down the length of **Addison Road**, past some large houses.

3 Turn left past **St Barnabas Church** into Melbury Road. Cross Abbotsbury Road and continue to the next road. Look out for the huge palm trees in the manicured garden on the corner. Turn sharp left here to reach the gates of **Holland Park**. Take the path ahead and walk through the arch. On the left is the **Ice House Gallery**.

Kyoto Gardens in Holland Park

Holland Park

1h30 — **3.25 MILES** **5.3 KM** **LEVEL 1 2 3**

WALK

Holland Park LONDON

4 Bear right through the hedged garden and, after passing through the end of the formal gardens, turn left signposted **'Kyoto Garden'** to follow the footpath as it descends a set of stone steps. The strange man you see with rolled-up sleeves walking towards you is, in fact, a realistic bronze sculpture. Once past him turn right.

5 At the end of this long fenced path turn second right along a long, straight path that heads slightly uphill, flanked by lime trees. Further on to the left is a **statue of Lord Holland** sitting high above a pond, the local watering hole for squirrels. If you're a keen birdwatcher, take a look in the woods behind the pond. Otherwise continue towards the junction of paths ahead and turn right.

MAP: AA Street by Street London

START/FINISH: Notting Hill Gate tube

PATHS: paved streets and tarmac paths

LANDSCAPE: exclusive properties and idyllic park

PUBLIC TOILETS: Holland Park and Notting Hill Gate

TOURIST INFORMATION: London, tel 020 7971 0027

THE PUB: The Ladbroke Arms, Notting Hill, W11

Getting to the start

Notting Hill Gate tube station can be a reached via the Central Line, the Circle Line and the District Line.

Researched and written by: Rebecca Harris, Deborah King

6 Soon go left and pass through a metal gate. Turn left along **Holland Walk**, a tarmac path also used by cyclists (if you turn right here you'll end up on Kensington High Street). Follow Holland Walk to the end.

7 Turn right and take the next right, **Aubrey Road**, which has an eclectic mix of architectural styles. (For **The Ladbroke Arms**, turn right then left along Ladbroke Grove, then first right into Ladbroke Road.) Follow Aubrey Road as it bends to the left and later passes **St George's Church**. At the crossroads continue ahead, turning into the first road on the left, **Hillgate Street**.

what to look for

If you turn right at the bronze sculpture of the walking man you will reach the Kyoto Garden, built to commemorate the friendship between Japan and Great Britain. It was erected for a Japanese festival in 1991. In the adjacent area are peacocks and if it's summertime, check what's showing at the open-air theatre – it may persuade you to return later.

8 After crossing **Hillgate Place** and its attractive rows of pastel-coloured terraced houses, turn right into **Notting Hill Gate** and back to the start.

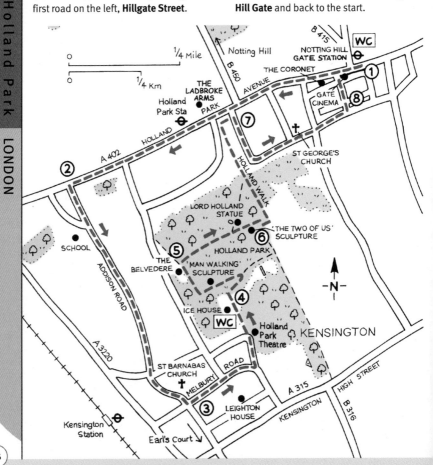

The Ladbroke Arms

One of London's trendier districts is the location of this pub, close to Holland Park and fashionable Notting Hill, renowned for its street market, chic restaurants and film location image. A broad spectrum of regulars is drawn to the chatty, civilised atmosphere, imaginative food and good ale and wine. There's a front terrace bursting with flowers – the scent wafts in on balmy summer days. Inside there are wooden floors, deep cream partially panelled walls with ginger hessian wall coverings, large etched mirrors and an array of pictures and prints. The raised eating area, up a few steps at the back, is really cosy.

Food

The menu changes daily and offers imaginative choices: confit of tuna with garlic lentils, soft boiled egg and bottarga, or prawns wrapped in betel leaves (miang gung) to start perhaps, followed by linguini with sweet tomato and basil, pan-fried salmon with prosciutto, or pea and mint risotto. Don't leave without trying the banana cake with mascarpone sorbet and custard, or the blood orange and chocolate parfait.

Family facilities

Children are very welcome inside the pub.

Alternative refreshment stops

You are definitely spoilt for choice around here. There's a café in the park, but if your budget allows, the Belvedere is pure decadence, not simply for the menu featuring fish and game but for the surroundings; it was once the grand ballroom of Holland House. There's also Il Carretto, an Italian restaurant in Hillgate Street.

☞ Where to go from here

Make the small detour to Leighton House in Holland Park Road. Inside this pre-Edwardian, red-brick exterior is an extensive collection of paintings, some by Lord Leighton, who was a president of the Royal Academy. The opulent Arab Hall is magnificent. It has a high ceiling and gilt mosaics and tiles. It's well worth a visit to see this alone. Take a stroll through nearby Kensington Gardens and visit the State Rooms in Kensington Palace to see some fine furnishings and works of art from the Royal Collection (www.hrp.org.uk).

about the pub

The Ladbroke Arms
54 Ladbroke Road,
Notting Hill
London W11 3NW
Tel: 020 7727 6648
www.capitalpubcompany.com

DIRECTIONS: off Ladbroke Grove, north of Holland Park Avenue. Nearest tube: Holland Park	
PARKING: none	
OPEN: daily; all day	
FOOD: daily	
BREWERY/COMPANY: free house	
REAL ALE: Greene King Abbot Ale and IPA, Fuller's London Pride, Adnams Bitter	
DOGS: well behaved dogs only	

Along the river and around Chelsea

in state before he was buried in St Paul's Cathedral), clothing and medical care.

Chelsea Pensioners are easily recognised by their unusual three-cornered hats and their scarlet coats, adorned with military medals. They are modelled on the red coats worn by British troops from the Civil War onwards and can have changed little since the Royal Hospital's foundation.

Battersea is the sort of park that has something for everyone. In the summer you'll hear anything from jazz music to the thud of a football, and see picnickers enjoying the sun. There's also another section of the Thames Path that runs alongside the river, with views over to the Chelsea Embankmentc and its constant flow of traffic. But over here it's different: it's peaceful and more than just a back garden for the Chelsea set.

Famed for its expensive properties, Chelsea is also home to the most famous pensioners in Britain.

Keeping up appearances

The Royal Hospital Chelsea was founded by Charles II and built in 1692 for veteran soldiers who had either served in the army for 20 years or been wounded. The minimum age for entry is now normally 65 and there is still accommodation for 500. Living here, the pensioner surrenders his army pension and in return receives a small room, all meals (taken in the spectacular Great Hall where the Duke of Wellington lay

the walk

1 From Sloane Square tube, cross the road ahead, then cross **Lower Sloane**

The large Buddhist Peace Pagoda in Battersea Park

The 19th-century Albert Bridge spans the Thames

2h00	3.25 MILES	5.3 KM	LEVEL 123

Street. Go past Peter Jones on the right and, a few paces on your left is the Duke of York's Headquarters with its café and square. Beyond this turn left into Cheltenham Terrace, then bear left into **Franklin's Row**.

2 At the bottom of Franklin's Row turn right along Royal Hospital Road. Just beyond the lawns on the right turn left into the hospital grounds at **Chelsea Gate**. A few paces further on the left, a gravel path leads to the Great Hall, chapel and museum. Continue to the end of the road and turn left on to some open grass. Now walk around the obelisk, to the gates on the far side of the grass. Leave through the gates with decorative urns to the **Chelsea Embankment**.

3 Turn right along the Embankment and right into **Tite Street**, where Oscar Wilde once lived. At the junction with Royal Hospital Road turn first left into Paradise Walk. The houses in this narrow, quiet road have window boxes and roof terraces. Turn right and then sharp left towards the Embankment (turn right to the **Chelsea Physic Garden** entrance). Turn right into the Embankment. (To reach the **Coopers Arms**, turn right up Flood Street at the junction with Royal Hospital Road.)

4 At the traffic lights cross Oakley Street and bear right by the beautiful *Boy with Dolphin* statue into narrow **Cheyne Walk**. Turn first right into Cheyne Row, where Thomas Carlyle lived. At the end turn left into Upper Cheyne Row, then left again into Lawrence Street – where there is a **plaque** to mark the Chelsea Porcelain Works – then

MAP: Explorer 161 London South
START/FINISH: Sloane Square tube; grid ref: AA Street by Street London: p.15 F7
PATHS: paved streets and tarmac paths
LANDSCAPE: mainly riverside views
PUBLIC TOILETS: Royal Hospital Chelsea Museum
TOURIST INFORMATION: London, tel 020 7971 0027
THE PUB: Coopers Arms, Chelsea, SW3
🛈 Sections of the walk are close to the river; keep children supervised

Getting to the start

Parking is difficult in the Sloane Street area. It is best accessed via the tube on either the Central or District lines. Sloane Street tube is one stop west of Victoria Station.

Researched and written by:
Rebecca Harris, Deborah King

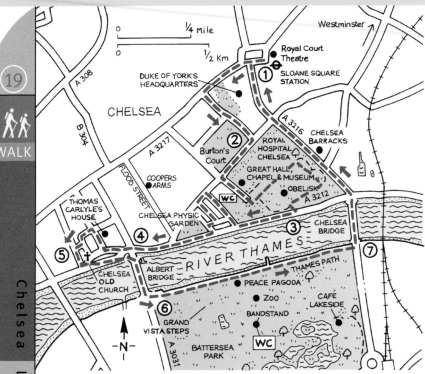

turn right into **Justice Walk**. (Don't be fooled
into thinking the sign of a red-robed judge
is a pub, it merely identifies where the old
courthouse used to be!)

5 Turn left into Old Church Street and
continue to the bottom of the street
with **Chelsea Old Church** on the left. Turn
left past the church and the statue of
Thomas More, who worshipped here. Walk
through Chelsea Embankment Gardens,
past the statue of Robert Carlyle and at the
junction with Oakley Street, cross the road
to the pink **Albert Bridge**.

6 Cross Albert Bridge and turn left at
the 'Riverside Walk' sign, through
the gate into **Battersea Park**. Bear left
and follow the riverside Thames Path,
past the Peace Pagoda in the park, along
to Chelsea Bridge.

7 Just before Chelsea Bridge, turn right
and then left at the road to leave the
park. Turn left again at the gates to cross
Chelsea Bridge. Continue ahead, over the
Embankment, passing **Chelsea Barracks**
on the right before joining Lower Sloane
Street. Turn right at **Sloane Square** to
retrace your steps back to Sloane
Square tube.

what to look for

Thomas Carlyle's terraced house in
Cheyne Row is typical of those built
at the time, but he was paranoid about the noise
from his neighbour's cockerels and spent 12 years
writing Frederick the Great (1858–65) from
his attic after blocking in the windows and
building a skylight.

The Coopers Arms

The Cooper's Arms is a quiet backstreet Chelsea pub close to the King's Road and the river. Here celebrities and the notorious rub shoulders with the aristocracy and locals in the bright, vibrant atmosphere, while the stuffed brown bear, Canadian moose and boar bring a character of their own to bar. The feel is open and airy – large windows, big station clock, wooden floor, simple wooden furniture – so nothing pretentious here, and the food is great. The modern pub menu offers freshly prepared food and includes organic eggs and meat from the landlord's Surrey farm. Free from intrusive music and electronic games, and with tip-top Young's ales and friendly staff, this is an excellent post-walk refreshment stop.

about the pub

Coopers Arms
87 Flood Street
London SW3 5TB
Tel: 020 7376 3120
www.thecoopers.co.uk

DIRECTIONS: Flood Street links the King's Road and Chelsea Embankment to the east of Albert Bridge. Nearest tube: Sloane Square	
PARKING: none	
OPEN: daily; all day	
FOOD: daily	
BREWERY/COMPANY: Young's Brewery	
REAL ALE: Young's Bitter and Special	
DOGS: welcome in the bar	

Food

The fresh, adventurous menu lists starters and light meals such as tomato and basil soup, and seared king scallops with chargrilled chorizo, crème fraiche and sweet chilli dressing, along with bangers and mash, pan-roasted sea bass with pesto oil, and spinach and ricotta tortellini with Napolitana sauce among the main course options.

Family facilities

Children are allowed inside (away from the bar) until 6pm.

Alternative refreshment stops

Try the Bar of the Royal Court Theatre adjacent to Sloane Street tube – it has an eclectic menu and some hearty dishes.

☞ Where to go from here

The Army Museum (www.national-army-museum.ac.uk) in the Royal Hospital Chelsea gives an insight into the life of a Chelsea Pensioner. Or go to South Kensington to explore the fascinating museum complex here. The choice includes the Victoria and Albert Museum (www.vam.ac.uk); the Natural History Museum (www.nhm.ac.uk); the Science Museum (www.sciencemuseum.org.uk).

From Battersea to Putney

Discover Thames-side London.

Battersea Park

It may not look very big on the map, but packed within its relatively small space there is much to see and do in Battersea Park. It attracts a wealth of wildlife; waterfowl regularly spotted on the lake include herons, cormorants, grebes and black swans. The park hosts a variety of cultural events, including a programme of outdoor concerts on summer evenings. There is also a funfair in summer. The Pump

Battersea Park – a haven among London's busy streets

House Gallery is housed in a restored Grade II-listed building, built in 1861 to supply water to the lakes and cascade of Battersea Park. Derelict for many years, it was restored and reopened in the early 1990s as a shop, park information centre and art gallery. Sports facilities are also on offer. London Recumbents offer a chance to try out their unusual cycles on the park's wide avenues, or you can hire a conventional bike to explore further afield.

A close-up view of the Pagoda in Battersea Park

the ride

1 From Rosary Gate head north up **Carriage Drive East**, with the deer enclosure and lake to your left. At The Parade turn left and ride along the wide traffic-free road; the Pagoda is to your left. Leave the park through Albert Bridge Gate and cross Albert Bridge Road to pick up Parkgate Road opposite – **The Prince Albert** pub is on the corner. At Battersea Bridge Road take a diagonal left along Westbridge Road. Look carefully for Granfield Street and turn left. Before you reach the college, look for the signed cycle route and turn right down an unpromising alleyway. This brings you into **Battersea High Street**; turn left here. Just beyond the railway turn right into Gwynne Road and take the first left into **Yelverton Road**.

2 Cross York Road on the crossing and pick up Wye Road on the other side. By the church follow the bend round into Ingrave Street. This turns into Fowler Court. At Plough Road turn left, and very soon pick up the **cycle-only right turn** into Maysoule Road. Turn left into Wynter Street. At the railway follow the signed path for cyclists to the right. Do not cross the railway; turn right into Petergate and left into **Eltringham Street**.

3 Use the toucan crossing to reach the other side of York Road, then bear left to cross **Bridgend Road**. Follow the shared pavement round by McDonald's to go up Smugglers Way. Keep straight ahead along the Causeway, despite the unpromising signs. You will soon find yourself at **The Spit**, a new nature reserve created at the

3h30 **9 MILES** **14 KM** **LEVEL 123**

MAP: OS Explorer 161 London South

START/FINISH: Rosary Gate, Battersea Park; grid ref: TQ 286770

TRAILS/TRACKS: suburban streets

LANDSCAPE: parkland, suburban streetscape

PUBLIC TOILETS: Battersea Park

TOURIST INFORMATION: London Line, tel 09068 663344

CYCLE HIRE: London Recumbents, Battersea Park, tel 020 7498 6543

THE PUB: The Prince Albert, Battersea, SW11

🚫 Sections of this ride involve cycling in traffic; they may not be suitable for the youngest children

Getting to the start

Battersea Park's Rosary Gate is reached from Queenstown Road, north of the A3205 Battersea Park Road. There is a pay-and-display car park in Battersea Park.

Why do this cycle ride?

This ride is less picturesque than others in this book, but there is plenty of interest en route to make up for that. Battersea Park alone has enough to occupy a family for hours, while Putney is a pleasant place to spend time and watch the world go by. The Spit at Wandsworth Creek provides an opportunity to see how wildlife is being nurtured in the centre of the city.

Researched and written by: James Hatts

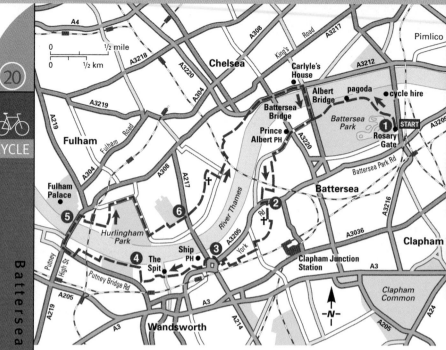

mouth of the River Wandle. Ride through the **industrial estate** to pick up Osiers Road. When this reaches the railway bridge at Point Pleasant turn right and head towards **the river**.

4 At the river pick up the well surfaced but **unsigned cycle track** and bear left. Soon you will reach the entrance to **Wandsworth Park**. It is necessary to dismount briefly as you leave the park to join Deodar Road. Keep straight ahead until the road bends to the left to join Putney Bridge Road. Bear right into **Putney High Street** and on to the bridge ahead.

5 Once over the bridge take the first right and follow **Ranelagh Gardens** under the railway viaduct. You need to skirt the perimeter of Hurlingham Park, so follow **Napier Avenue** to the left, turning right into Hurlingham Road at the north-western corner of the park. Head back south

towards the river along Broomhouse Road, but before the end take a left into Sulivan Road. Bear right into Peterborough Road, but almost immediately there is a left turn along a **segregated cycle track** along the bottom end of South Park.

6 Take care as you cross Wandsworth Bridge Road to pick up Stephenson Road on the other side. At the **Catholic church** bear right into Elswick Street. Turn right into Bagley's Lane at the end. At Townmead Road turn left and approach the **Chelsea Harbour complex**. Beyond the roundabout keep straight ahead and go under the railway, picking up Harbour Avenue on the other side. Turn left at the next roundabout, then bear right along Lots Road, past the former London Underground **power station**. Keep straight ahead when Lots Road joins Cheyne Walk. Return south using **Albert Bridge** and back to the start through the park via the outward route.

The Prince Albert

The Prince Albert stands opposite the Albert Gate to Battersea Park. This smart pub has been refurbished to a high standard and attracts a mixed clientele of locals and visitors to the park. The patio is tucked away behind the pub and offers ample seating, with large umbrellas and patio heaters for cooler days.

Food
The menu ranges from 'snacking plates' such as tomato and pesto bruschetta or savoury cheesecake to battered fish and fries or Jamaican jerk chicken. Rustic bread sandwiches with hot fillings in a rosemary and sea-salt pain-rustique are a popular choice. On Sundays a traditional roast is served.

Family facilities
Children are welcome throughout the pub.

Alternative refreshment stops
There are cafés in Battersea Park and numerous pubs along the route, notably the Lots Road Pub & Dining Room.

☛ Where to go from here
Cross the Thames to Chelsea and take the children to the Chelsea World of Sport (www.chelseaworldofsport.com) on the Fulham Road. This interactive sports attraction has over 30 exhibits that will challenge visitors of all ages. There are 'interactive coaches' on hand to improve your performance and you can test your skill and compare yourself against the professionals at football, sprinting and volleyball. Just across Albert Bridge is Thomas Carlyle's House in Cheyne Row. This Queen Anne town house contains the historian and writer's books, portraits and personal relics, and has a lovely walled garden (www.nationaltrust.org.uk).

about the pub

The Prince Albert
85 Albert Bridge Road, Battersea
London SW11 4PF
Tel: 020 7228 0923
www.theprincealbert.com

DIRECTIONS: on the west side of the park, on the corner of Albert Bridge Road and Parkgate Road

PARKING: pay and display in Battersea Park, including at Rosary Gate and opposite the pub

OPEN: daily; all day

FOOD: daily; all day

BREWERY/COMPANY: free house

REAL ALE: changing guest beers

Around Balham

A circular route highlighting the greener spots of Balham and its most famous art deco property.

Huguenots and Hitler

Balham is mentioned in the Domesday Book. In the late 18th century it consisted mainly of fields peppered with large houses. In the 1860s, by the time the railway network had increased, it was already popular with the working and middle classes and residential developments began to appear. In the 1930s the architect G Kay Green designed the largest privately owned block under one roof in Europe. Du Cane Court, named after a family of Huguenots on whose land the site was built, contains 676 flats and is home to more than 1,000 residents. When World War Two began many people left for the relative safety of the countryside, but the Foreign Office came to the rescue: many of its staff rented a flat in the block, no doubt impressed by the short train journey to Victoria. In the 1940s a small flat cost around £6 a month to rent, which was not considered cheap, but it included a remarkable view. Today, from the

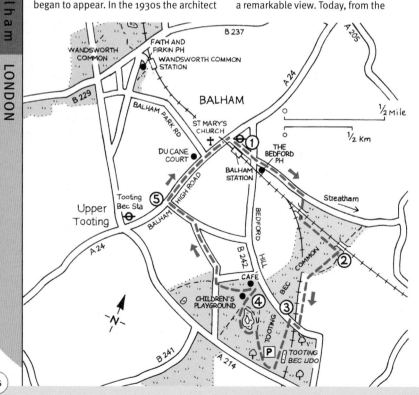

seventh-floor rooftop, the panoramic view over London must surely match those from Parliament Hill, Alexandra Palace, Canary Wharf and anywhere else north of the river, for that matter.

Despite being a major landmark in the area, because of its size, it was never bombed by the Germans during the war (although 64 lives were lost when Balham Station was hit). Some even say that Hitler had placed spies here and that it was used as a landmark by his aircrews. If this were true, the spies would have been in good hands for, food rations permitting, the restaurant on the top floor served some very fine dishes.

Margaret Rutherford, the comedy actress who became a household name after starring as Miss Marple was born here in 1892. Also born here, but in 1946, was John Sullivan, who wrote *Citizen Smith* and the timeless *Only Fools and Horses* for television. If you want to see the interior of Du Cane Court, you'll have to watch one of the Agatha Christie adaptations in which the lobby and flats have been featured; the sweeping art deco staircase is indeed a rare and wonderful sight.

the walk

1 Turn right at **Balham Station**, along Balham Station Road. Cross at the lights, passing **The Bedford** pub, into Fernlea Road. At a mini-roundabout turn right before a strip of common and go under a **railway bridge**. Turn left and follow the wall of the railway embankment, passing a **playground** and playing fields on the right.

MAP: OS Explorer 161 London South
START/FINISH: Balham Station; grid ref: TQ 285731
PATHS: paved streets, tarmac and gravel paths across commons
LANDSCAPE: urban streets and commons
PUBLIC TOILETS: Tooting Bec Common
TOURIST INFORMATION: London, tel 020 7971 0027
THE PUB: The Bedford, Balham, SW12

Getting to the start

Balham Station is on the A24 between Collier's Wood and Clapham Common. There is no public car park and street parking is severely restricted, but you could try the pay-and-display in Fernlea Road. Balham Station is on both the tube's Northern Line and the National Rail network.

Researched and written by:
Leigh Hatts, Deborah King

2 At another bridge take the right-hand **tarmac path** running parallel to a row of houses. As the path bends to the left, it runs alongside another railway track lined with trees before meeting a road, Bedford Hill. Turn right and cross the road to join a path on the left at **Tooting Bec Common**.

3 After a few yards turn sharp left on a rough path that at first hugs the railway track and then passes **Tooting Bec Lido**. Pass the Lido car park and follow the path

that circles it clockwise. After crossing the car park approach road, take the right-hand path leading into the common and, at a **clump of trees**, turn left along a narrow gravel path around a lake.

4 At a tarmac path go right and beyond the children's playground take the next left to the café and follow this path until you reach **Doctor Johnson Avenue**. Turn right past the entrance to Hillbury Road and go over the crossroads into Manville Road. At the next crossroads turn left into Ritherdon Road and continue to the end.

5 Turn right at the traffic lights into **Balham High Road**, passing Du Cane Court and St Mary's Church before reaching the station where the walk began.

Tooting Bec Lido is one of England's biggest open-air swimming pools

what to look for

Hamilton House, on the right of Balham High Road, is the Polish White Eagle Club, used by many of Balham's Polish immigrants who settled here after World War Two. On the opposite side of the road is the red-brick Polish Catholic church, Christ the King.

The Bedford

The now legendary Bedford is a comfortable, airy sort of pub with two spacious bars, deep sofas, a huge stone fireplace, wood panelled walls, cosy corners and decent London-brewed ales on tap. During the week it operates as a pub, but at weekends it turns into one of London's premier comedy clubs, favoured by both comics and punters. The quirky theatre is balconied, with an ornate, domed ceiling and tables in the intimate 'overflow' room decorated with candles. When the laughter ends it turns into a nightclub until 2am.

Food

Lighter bites include the Bedford breakfast (lunch only), grilled rib-eye steak sandwich with onion marmalade and mustard mayonnaise, roast tomato and ginger soup, and steamed mussels with garlic and cream. Main meals range from lemon thyme risotto and the Balham burger to grilled salmon with lemon and fennel salad, and calves' liver and bacon with spring onion mash.

Family facilities

Children are welcome in the pub until 6pm.

Alternative refreshment stops

The café on Tooting Bec Common serves all-day breakfasts, burgers, and sausage and chips.

☛ Where to go from here

During the summer months, if your lungs are strong, take your swimming gear on the walk and visit the gigantic Tooting Bec Lido where even one width of the pool is a breathtaking 108ft (33m). Lidos are larger

about the pub

The Bedford
77 Bedford Hill, Balham
London SW12 9HD
Tel: 020 8682 8940
www.thebedford.co.uk

DIRECTIONS: on the corner of Bedford Hill and Fernlea Road (on walk just after Point 1). Nearest tube: Balham

PARKING: none

OPEN: daily; all day

FOOD: daily

BREWERY/COMPANY: free house

REAL ALES: Fuller's London Pride, Young's Bitter

DOGS: welcome inside

WALK

Balham LONDON

than life and this one, with its endearing wooden cubicle doors painted in bright, Caribbean shades, is no exception. On a hot summer's day it can get as many as 6,000 visitors.

Regent's Park

Rose gardens, an open-air theatre, panoramic views from Primrose Hill, birdsong along the Regent's Canal and Little Venice.

Regent's Park

'I must go seek some dew-drops here
And hang a pearl in every cowslip's ear'

So sings the Fairy to Puck in *A Midsummer Night's Dream*, William Shakespeare's romantic fantasy. If you think that romance is dead, you need to try this walk, especially on weekdays, when it's quieter. Along these canals you'll see barges rather than gondolas, but on a fine, balmy day you can return to Regent's Park in the evening to see a performance at the magical open-air theatre, and there isn't one of those in Venice.

'It shall be called Bottom's Dream because it hath no bottom...' wrote Shakespeare. In a similar way, this walk was John Nash's dream because, in 1820 when he designed the area, it was the grandest piece of town planning ever devised in central London and has not been matched since. His scheme was based on a park peppered with large villas that looked like separate mansions, but which actually consisted of more than 20 houses. Sprinkle on to this some grand terraces and the result is idyllic Regent's Park and its little sister, Primrose Hill, from where the views are exhilarating.

If you're lucky enough to find that *A Midsummer Night's Dream* is on at the open-air theatre, don't expect it to be one of Shakespeare's best stories, for it's about ideas rather than plot. 'The course of true love never runs smooth' explained the bard and this concept carries on throughout the play. Since the play was first published in 1600 it has been the source of inspiration for countless stories of tiny fairies living in the woods. Walt Disney made a fortune from the idea, but it didn't entertain the prominent diarist Samuel Pepys, who saw it in 1662 for the first time and wrote: '...nor shall I ever (see it) again, for it is the most insipid ridiculous play that I ever saw in my life.'

Had Pepys seen it in the unique setting of Regent's Park, however, he might have thought differently. He could have arrived early to picnic and drink champagne on the lawn, and afterwards taken a stroll to Primrose Hill . Try it one midsummer's day and if this little potion doesn't bring some magic into your life, you'll have to ask Puck for some help.

the walk

1 Take the north exit from Baker Street tube and turn right, along **Baker Street**. Cross the road ahead via two sets of pedestrian lights, and carry straight on, turning right, across another road via more pedestrian lights to enter **Regent's Park**. Turn right. Cross the bridge over the lake and then bear left, past the **bandstand**.

2 Turn left when you reach the Inner Circle road. Beyond **The Holme** turn left, through the metal gates, then turn immediately right. At the next fork take the right path as it bears round to the right, past a **large house**. Turn right at a crossing of paths,

1h30   **3.25 MILES**   **5.3 KM**   **LEVEL 1 2 3**

continuing straight over the next junction to meet the **Broad Walk** with benches.

3 Turn left into the Broad Walk. Continue straight along this wide walkway, past the café on the left, past the impressive Indian drinking fountain and past **London Zoo**. At the Outer Circle cross the road and continue ahead over a canal bridge to **Prince Albert Road**.

4 At Prince Albert Road, turn left and a few paces on cross the road at the pedestrian lights to enter a corner entrance of **Primrose Hill**. Take the right-hand path and follow it uphill to the **viewpoint**.

5 Follow the path that bears left, leading downhill, to join a straight path that leads back to **Prince Albert Road**. Cross at the zebra crossing and turn right, then almost immediately left down a **footpath**.

Top: Regent's Park
Below: Penguins in the zoo in Regent's Park

MAP: AA Street by Street London

START: Baker Street tube

FINISH: Warwick Avenue tube

PATHS: paved streets and tarmac paths

LANDSCAPE: exclusive properties and idyllic park

PUBLIC TOILETS: none on route

TOURIST INFORMATION: Camden, tel 020 7974 5974

THE PUB: The Prince Alfred & Formosa Dining Room, Little Venice

🛈 Take care alongside the canal

Getting to the start

Baker Street tube station is easily accessed via the Hammersmith & City Line, the Jubilee Line, the Circle Line and the Metropolitan Line.

Researched and written by:
Rebecca Harris, Deborah King

6 Don't cross the bridge, but turn right along a hedge-lined path that bends sharply to the left on to the **upper tow path**. Turn right and follow the tow path for 0.5 mile (800m). The banks of the canal are overhung with weeping willows, and palatial homes line this stretch of the walk. Continue ahead under the **railway bridges** – less enchanting but rest assured that better things lie ahead – and, after a few paces, you'll pass the **houseboats** moored at Lisson Green before a tow path tunnel.

7 As the canal disappears under another tunnel, walk up a steep slope on the right. Cross over the road and turn first left along the continuation of the tow path, past residential houses on the right to **Aberdeen Place**. At the end cross Maida Vale and follow Blomfield Road all the way to **Little Venice**. Cross Warwick Avenue and follow the road as it bends to the right,

what to look for

Regent's Park's Open Air Theatre was founded in 1932 and is the premier professional outdoor theatre in Great Britain. Many well-known artists have appeared here during the summer season including Deborah Kerr, Vivian Leigh, Felicity Kendal, Jeremy Irons and Maria Aitken. With seating for well over 1,000, it's larger than the Barbican and the Olivier Theatre on the South Bank.

past the footbridge. Turn right into Warwick Place and then left again to find Warwick Avenue tube 100yds (91m) ahead. For the pub continue along Warwick Avenue, cross **Clifton Gardens** and take the second right into Formosa Street. **The Prince Alfred** is at the junction with Castellain Road and Warrington Crescent.

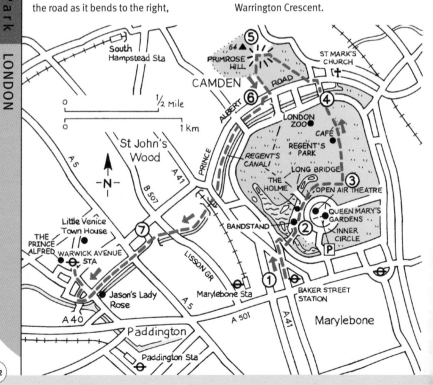

The Prince Alfred & Formosa Dining Room

Affectionately known as the PA, this favoured Little Venice watering-hole was built in 1863 and is one of the few pubs in the capital that retains its ornate Victorian décor, notably the carved gilt and wood bar, huge sculpted ceilings, frosted glass, original tiling and unusual, midget-sized doorways linking the five partitioned sections of the bar. You can book one of the areas or the 'snug' for friends with no charge. Simple leather sofas on wooden floors, excellent wines by the glass, summer cocktails and modern pub food make it a great place to relax. The restaurant, with its glass ceiling, leather bench seating and wooden tables and chairs, is understated chic.

about the pub

The Prince Alfred & Formosa Dining Room
5A Formosa Street
London W9 1EE
Tel: 020 7286 3287
www.thespiritgroup.com

DIRECTIONS: nearest tube: Warwick Avenue	
PARKING: none	
OPEN: daily; all day	
FOOD: daily	
BREWERY/COMPANY: Spirit Group	
REAL ALE: Fuller's London Pride	
DOGS: allowed inside	

Food

The eclectic modern pub menu may include roast tomato soup, Cumberland sausages with mash and onion gravy, calves' liver with Savoy cabbage, bacon and parsley mash, or roast cod with sauce vierge for lunch. There are additional evening dishes such as sea bass on bok choy (pak choi) with sweet chilli dressing and lamb rump with red wine jus. Good puddings and an excellent-value two-course lunch menu are also available.

Family facilities

Children are welcome inside. Smaller portions and high chairs are provided.

Alternative refreshment stops

Just a few paces from Warwick Avenue tube lies the Little Venice Town House in Warrington Crescent. It was here that Alan Turing, the mathematician responsible for breaking the Enigma code during World War Two, was born in 1912. Pop in for afternoon tea after the walk.

☞ Where to go from here

Don't miss London Zoo where children can come face-to-face with some of the hairiest, scariest, tallest and smallest animals on the planet. It is home to over 12,000 animals, insects, reptiles and fish. There are interactive displays, a Children's Zoo with farmyard animals you can touch.

Around Hyde Park

Discover a green oasis in the heart of the capital.

Hyde Park

Henry VIII and his court once hunted deer in Hyde Park; the Tudor monarch acquired the land from the monks of Westminster Abbey in 1536. Public access was first permitted under James I, but it was Charles I who opened the park fully to the general public in 1637. During the Great Plague in 1665 many Londoners set up camp in the park, hoping to escape the disease. The Serpentine – the vast ornamental lake dominating the park – was created in the 1730s by Queen Caroline, wife of George II.

The latest in Hyde Park's long line of royal connections is the controversial £3.6 million Diana, Princess of Wales Memorial Fountain, unveiled by the Queen in 2004. The fountain was designed by US architect Kathryn Gustafson, and is based on an oval stone ring. Water enters the fountain at its highest point, then bounces down steps. It picks up momentum and is invigorated by jets. As it flows westwards it resembles a babbling brook. Air bubbles are added as it approaches a waterfall before entering a water feature. Water from east and west meets at the reflecting pool, before being pumped out to restart the cycle.

the ride

1 From the West Carriage Drive car park, opposite the **Serpentine Gallery**, cross the road and join the cycle track on the pavement on the west side of West Carriage

Safe, traffic-free cycling in Hyde Park in the heart of London

CYCLE

1h00 **2.5 MILES** **4 KM** **LEVEL 1**23

Hyde Park LONDON

MAP: OS Explorer 173 London North

START/FINISH: West Carriage Drive car park; grid ref: TQ 269800

TRAILS/TRACKS: well-surfaced paths

LANDSCAPE: urban parkland

PUBLIC TOILETS: in the park

TOURIST INFORMATION: London Line, tel 09068 663344

CYCLE HIRE: London Bicycle Tour Company, 1a Gabriels Wharf, 56 Upper Ground, SE1, tel 020 7928 6838

THE PUB: The Wilton Arms, Kinnerton Street

⚠ Be sure to give priority to pedestrians on shared-use paths. Beware of unpredictable rollerbladers!

Getting to the start

The West Carriage Drive car park is south of the bridge over the Serpentine. It can be approached from the A402 Bayswater Road to the north or the A315 Kensington Gore/Kensington Road to the south. The pay-and-display car park is open 8.30am-6.30pm.

Why do this cycle ride?

An ideal ride for families with very young children, this is a chance to make the most of a huge expanse of green space that Londoners often forget they have on their doorstep. Glance to your left as you cross the Serpentine Bridge and you'd never guess that you were in the heart of the capital. Yet elsewhere there are surprising views of familiar London landmarks.

Researched and written by: James Hatts

Drive. The Diana, Princess of Wales **Memorial Fountain** is on your right.

2 The track drops down on to the road to cross the **Serpentine bridge**. Once across be sure to look out for the point where the path resumes on the pavement, as the cycle lane on the road surface stops abruptly.

3 At Victoria Gate cross the road and follow the cycle path along **The Ring**. The path here is on the road, but it is often traffic-free.

4 As you approach Cumberland Gate and Marble Arch, look for the **cycle route sign** for Chelsea Bridge and cross the road to pick up the cycle path on **Broad Walk**. You may need to reduce speed here

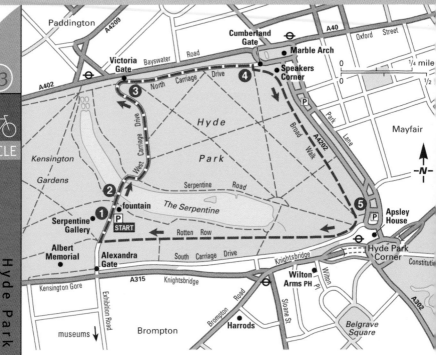

as the cycle lane can be obstructed by crowds milling around at **Speakers' Corner**. It then heads south on Broad Walk, a pleasant, wide, tree-lined boulevard.

5 On the approach to **Queen Elizabeth Gate** at Hyde Park Corner, follow signs to the right for **Rotten Row** to return to the car park at West Carriage Drive. If heading

for **The Wilton Arms** pub, you will need to leave the park through this gate. On Rotten Row, keep to the left on this fairly narrow path shared with pedestrians and rollerbladers. At West Carriage Drive, use the pedestrian crossing and pick up the cycle track again on the west side in front of the **Serpentine Gallery**. (This simple circular ride can be easily extended eastwards with a foray along **Constitution Hill**'s excellent parallel cycle track to see Buckingham Palace, or to the west to explore Kensington Gardens. Notices at the park entrances show where cycling is currently permitted.)

The Serpentine in Hyde Park

The Wilton Arms

Exuberant hanging baskets and window boxes decorate this early 19th-century pub, and a tasteful conservatory occupies the garden, so arrive early to ensure a seat in summer. Inside, high settles and bookcases create cosy individual seating areas, all fully air-conditioned. Owned by Shepherd Neame, Britain's oldest brewer, it was named after the 1st Earl Wilton and is known locally as the 'Village Pub'.

Food
The chalkboard menu lists the house speciality – a doorstep sandwich of salt roast beef with horseradish and mustard dressing. There's also beef and Guinness pie, fish and chips, lamb hotpot and a choice of curries, alongside staples such as burgers and ploughman's meals.

Family facilities
Children are welcome inside the bar if they are eating, and smaller portions of main menu dishes can be ordered.

Alternative refreshment stops
You will find various cafés and kiosks in Hyde Park.

☛ Where to go from here
Along the ride, stop off at Apsley House, The Wellington Museum at Hyde Park Corner, the 19th-century home of the first Duke of Wellington. From West Carriage Drive you are within walking distance of the South Kensington museums. Spend some time at the Victoria and Albert Museum (www.vam.ac.uk), the Natural History Museum (www.nhm.ac.uk) or the Science Museum (www.sciencemuseum.org.uk). Explore Kensington Gardens and visit the restored Kings Apartments in Kensington Palace (www.hrp.org.uk). The Serpentine Gallery has fascinating changing exhibitions of contemporary art (www.serpentinegallery.org).

about the pub

The Wilton Arms
71 Kinnerton Street
London SW1X 8ER
Tel: 020 7235 4854

DIRECTIONS: tucked away behind Knightsbridge and best accessed from Wilton Place. From the Queen Elizabeth Gate of Hyde Park, leave the park and cross to the other side of Knightsbridge. Turn right, and continue until you reach Wilton Place, Turn left here, and take the next right. You will soon spot the pub

PARKING: none

OPEN: daily; all day

FOOD: all day; no food Sunday

BREWERY/COMPANY: Shepherd Neame

REAL ALE: Shepherd Neame Goldings, Spitfire and Master Brew

Through Mayfair

A leisurely walk through wealthy Mayfair in the style of James Bond.

007 in Mayfair

When the author Ian Fleming created the character James Bond he paved the way for a small minority of actors to participate in an adventure that would take them to some of the world's most exotic locations. Fleming's first novel, *Casino Royale*, published in 1953, introduced the tough, romantic, handsome hero who became affectionately known as 007. This walk captures some of the glamour of James Bond, but you must go armed with a good imagination.

Mayfair was developed in the 18th century, predominantly by the wealthy Grosvenor family. It is one of the most elegant areas in London. Many of its exclusive shops bear coats of arms, denoting that they are official suppliers to the royal family, and the locality is peppered with superb hotels and restaurants – this is the type of place in which 007 would feel quite at home. In fact 'home' could be Albany, a covert block of bachelors' apartments. It was created from a town house owned by George III's son, who was popularised in the nursery rhyme 'The Grand Old Duke of York'. From here 007 would visit Old Bond Street and its cluster of exclusive shops selling jewellery (Tiffany and Cartier) and pens (Mont Blanc), and also South Audley Street, for this is where the royal gunmaker Purdey's is to be found. A few doors away, the Spy Shop is where Q might have spent many a fine hour. He may have recommended the recording briefcase

with concealed microphones that optionally transmits conversation, or perhaps the body wires or transmitting pens and calculators from this shop that sells 'business tools built to military specification'.

For relaxation, 007 could head for the Elemis Day Spa. There, for an hour or so, he would be transported to a world of sensory heaven in either the Thai, Moorish or Balinese suites, for some serious cleansing and massage in exotic surroundings. Feeling refreshed, he may then even stop off at the Kenneth Turner flower shop in Avery Row and treat the long-suffering Miss Moneypenny to an artistic bouquet. Then, assuming he was not on a case, off he'd go to Claridge's hotel in search of his favourite tipple.

If you're following in the footsteps of 007, apart from never saying never again, how can you go to Claridge's Bar and not order such a legendary cocktail?

the walk

1 Turn into pedestrianised **South Molton Street**, which is alongside the Oxford Street entrance to Bond Street Station. At the end turn left into Brook Street. Cross the road and turn right down a cobbled alley, **Lancashire Court**, which opens into a courtyard where you will find Hush restaurant. Beyond an archway is the **Elemis Day Spa**.

2 Turn left here to reach New Bond Street. Go left and right by Fenwick's into Brook Street. At the **statue** of the young William Pitt in Hanover Square turn right into St George Street, past **St George's Church** and left at the end into Conduit Street.

1h30 — 2.75 MILES — 4.4 KM — LEVEL 1 23

3 Take the next right into the road of fine suits, **Savile Row**. At the end bear left and then right into Sackville Street. Turn right along Piccadilly and look out for the entrance to **Albany's courtyard**.

4 Just past the auspicious-looking **Burlington Arcade** turn right into Old Bond Street and past several exclusive shops, including those of Cartier, Mont Blanc and Tiffany. Turn left after Asprey & Garrard into **Grafton Street**, which takes a 90-degree left bend, becoming Dover Street.

5 Turn right down **Hay Hill** and at the junction cross the road to Starbucks, then go right towards **Berkeley Square**.

Top: Georgian houses on Berkeley Square
Below: Grosvenor Square

MAP: AA Street by Street London
START/FINISH: Bond Street tube
PATHS: paved streets
LANDSCAPE: shopping, residential and business district of West End
PUBLIC TOILETS: none on route
TOURIST INFORMATION: London, tel 020 7971 0027
THE PUB: The Audley, 41–43 Mount Street, W1

Getting to the start
Bond Street Station is on the tube's Central and Jubilee lines.

Researched and written by:
Leigh Hatts, Deborah King

Mayfair

LONDON

Turn left along the bottom of the square to reach handsome Charles Street. Beyond the **Chesterfield Hotel** turn left along Queen Street and then right into **Curzon Street**.

6 Turn right into South Audley Street and at the Spy Shop and Purdey's (gunmakers) turn left into Mount Street. At the end turn right along Park Lane, past the **Grosvenor House Hotel**.

7 Turn right into Upper Grosvenor Street, past the **American Embassy** and through Grosvenor Square, then left into Davies Street. Next, take the first right into **Brooks Mews** and go left along the narrow

Avery Row. This brings you on to Brook Street. From here you can retrace your steps along **South Molton Street**, back to Bond Street Station where the walk began.

what to look for

Decadence – while you might not see many Aston Martins there will be some Mercedes, BMWs and Audis despite the congestion charge. Similarly, the shops in this area of London are some of the most exclusive in the city. Enter these and you'll have the door opened for you by a man in a dark suit.

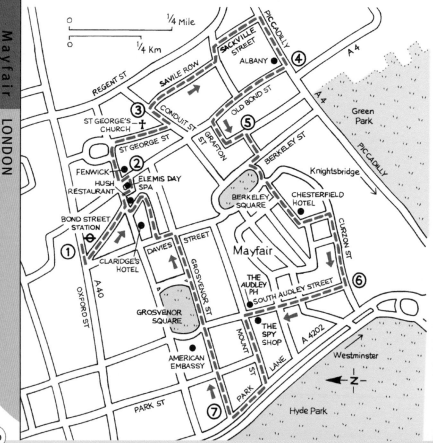

The Audley

The Audley is an immaculate, late Victorian pub with an opulent façade adorned with pretty pale pink terracotta tiles and intricate ironwork. Add large arched windows, tumbling ivy and colourful flowers boxes and the Audley fits nicely into this refined Mayfair street, with its neighbouring classy restaurants and shops. The interior is equally smart, with original chandeliers, ornate plaster ceilings, plush leather upholstery, cosy alcove seating and old Mayfair prints on the walls, and attracts an up market clientele. The long hardwood bar serves Young's and Fuller's ales, and there's a good selection of traditional English dishes.

Food

This pub takes its food seriously. There are no sandwiches – instead traditional dishes include home-made pies, fish and chips, sausages and mash, filled jacket potatoes, and calves' liver and bacon, along with puddings such as apple pie and strawberry shortcake.

Family facilities

Children welcome until 5pm. There are seats outside on the pavement.

Alternative refreshment stops

There are coffee bars and sandwich shops in Bond Street Station.

☞ Where to go from here

Take the Central Line tube to Tottenham Court Road and stroll to the British Museum in Great Russell Street (www.thebritishmuseum.ac.uk). It was founded in 1753 and is one of the greatest museums in the world, with displays covering the works of humanity from prehistoric to modern times. It offers gallery talks, guided tours and lectures, and young visitors can enjoy special children's trails.

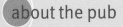

about the pub

The Audley
41–43 Mount Street
London W1
Tel: 020 7499 1843

DIRECTIONS: Mount Street is off Park Lane and the pub is close to South Audley Street, opposite Purdey's Gun Shop. Nearest tube: Bond Street or Green Park

PARKING: very limited street parking

OPEN: daily; all day

FOOD: daily; all day

BREWERY/COMPANY: Spirit Group

REAL ALE: Fuller's London Pride, Young's Bitter

DOGS: not allowed inside

Mayfair LONDON

From St James's Park to Kensington Gardens

A healthy, linear walk from St James's Park to Kensington Gardens.

Nash to the rescue

St James's Park, the oldest of the Royal Parks, started life as a swamp, but Henry VIII started the changes. Charles II made it look as much like Versailles as possible and around 150 years later the architect John Nash replaced the French layout with the English one that you see today. The contrast of Green Park may be what's needed if you prefer a less manicured environment.

In Hyde Park there are lime trees, rose gardens and the Serpentine, a lake on which you can usually take a boat. Kensington Gardens is on the other side of the Serpentine Bridge and here you'll pass the gates in front of Kensington Palace.

the walk

1 From Charing Cross Station turn left into the **Strand** and left again into Northumberland Street. Bear left along Northumberland Avenue and, after a few paces, cross over into **Great Scotland Yard**, with the Nigerian Embassy on the corner.

St James's Park on a sunny day

2 As the road bears right turn left into Whitehall, cross to the other side and head for the arch of **Horse Guards Parade**, where the guards are on duty for an hour at a time. Go through the arch leading to a gravel square used for the Trooping the Colour ceremony in June.

3 At the far side of Horse Guards enter **St James's Park** to the left of the Guards Monument. Turn left following the path along the end of the lake. At the junction of paths turn right and take the right fork. Continue along this path by the lakeside, past weeping willow trees, to a **blue bridge**.

4 Cross the bridge, stopping half-way across to enjoy the views: westwards is Buckingham Palace and eastwards is Horse Guards Parade, where the skyline looks almost fairytale-like. Turn left, past the **Nash Shrubberies**, and leave the park on the right. Cross The Mall, walk around the monument of Queen Victoria and enter **Green Park** through the impressive gates by Constitution Hill.

5 With your back to the gates take the straight walkway, with benches, slightly to the left. Continue up the long path, past a **water sculpture** to the left, to the end at Piccadilly. Still inside the park, turn left at the end and continue up the slight incline that leads to **Hyde Park Corner**.

6 Use the underpass ahead to first reach the central island and Wellington Arch, and then Hyde Park itself. (For **The**

The tree-lined St James Park with government buildings in the distance

2h30 | **4.25 MILES** | **6.8 KM** | **LEVEL 1**23

MAP:	OS Explorer 173 London North
START:	Charing Cross tube; grid ref: TQ 303803
FINISH:	High Street Kensington tube; grid ref: TQ 255794
PATHS:	mainly tarmac paths through the parks
LANDSCAPE:	parkland with occasional busy road and hum of traffic
PUBLIC TOILETS:	in each park
TOURIST INFORMATION:	London, tel 020 7971 0027
THE PUB:	The Grenadier, Belgravia, SW1

Getting to the start

Charing Cross railway station and tube can be reached via the Northern and Bakerloo lines and from mainline stations in south east London and beyond. There's a car park in St Martin's Lane.

Researched and written by:
Rebecca Harris, Deborah King

WALK

St James's Park   LONDON

Grenadier pub, exit the underpass on the south side of Knightsbridge, then turn left along Wilton Crescent which leads into Wilton Row.) Go over the crossing on **Rotten Row**, and follow the left-hand path, bearing right through a rose garden with a dolphin fountain. Continue straight on, walking slightly downhill through a small metal gate, bearing right to reach the Dell Restaurant beside the **Serpentine**.

what to look for

Just across the Blue Bridge in St James's Park is an area called the Nash Shrubberies. It has been restored to Nash's original, 'floriferous' specifications, with an emphasis on foliage.

7 Continue over a junction of paths bearing left, along the northern edge of the Serpentine, past the **boat houses** to reach the Serpentine Bridge. Pass underneath it and up some steps on the right. Turn right, crossing over the bridge to enter Kensington Gardens. Take the middle path and continue ahead, ignoring other paths. When you join the **cycling pat**h turn right and head towards Kensington Palace, with a **bandstand** on the left and a pond on the right.

8 Carry on over a junction and bear left along the path that runs to the left of the gates to the **Kensington Palace** state apartments. At the end turn left to reach Kensington High Street. Turn right to pass the Royal Garden Hotel, Kensington Church Street and cross **Kensington High Street** to the tube station on the left.

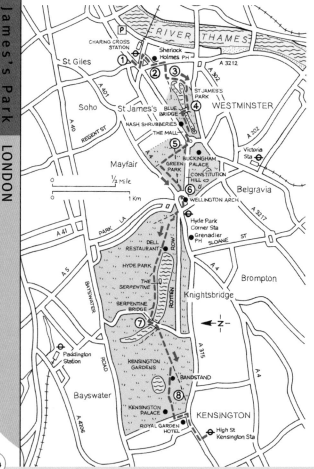

The Grenadier

The bright red, white and blue frontage of the patriotic Grenadier, regularly used for films and television series, can't be missed. Once the Duke of Wellington's officers' mess and much frequented by King George IV, it stands in a quiet cobbled mews behind Hyde Park Corner and remains largely undiscovered by tourists. The dark interior (candlelit even in summer) features dark wood panelling, wooden floors, heavy red curtains, cosy winter fires and the place is full of historical atmosphere with sabres, daggers, bugles and bearskins decorating the intimate bar. Outside is the remaining stone of the Duke's mounting block, and beside the little blue double doors there's even a sentry box.

Food

Dishes range from black pudding stack, and spinach and Roquefort tart starters, to minted lamb shoulder, duck in red wine and chicken breast with thyme dumplings

Family facilities

Children are welcome in the restaurant area only, where smaller portions of adult dishes are available.

Alternative refreshment stops

The Sherlock Holmes in Northumberland Avenue serves its own label ale as well as Flowers and London Pride, and there are cafés in the parks.

☞ Where to go from here

The views from the fourth-floor balcony of Wellington Arch (www.english-heritage.org.uk) into the gardens of Buckingham Palace and along Constitution Hill are worth the small admission price alone. Arrive around 11.30am or 12.30pm and you'll see the Household Cavalry trotting past, on their way back to their barracks. Visit the State Apartments in Kensington Palace (www.hrp.org.uk), or spend some time at one or more of London's finest museums in South Kensington – the Victoria and Albert Museum (www.vam.ac.uk), the Natural History Museum (www.nhm.ac.uk) or the Science Museum (wwwsciencemuseum.org.uk).

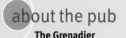

about the pub

The Grenadier
18 Wilton Row
Belgrave Square
London SW1 7NR
Tel: 020 7235 3074
www.thespiritgroup.com

DIRECTIONS: off Knightsbridge just west of Hyde Park Corner. Wilton Crescent leads to Wilton Row. Nearest tube: Hyde Park Corner

PARKING: none

OPEN: daily; all day

FOOD: daily

BREWERY/COMPANY: Spirit Group

REAL ALE: Young's Bitter, Fuller's London Pride, Wells Bombardier, Courage Best

DOGS: not allowed inside

Westminster to Smithfield

A look at some of the city's landmarks, from Whitehall through to Smithfield.

Corridors of power

The walk begins across the square from Westminster Abbey. On a corner opposite Horse Guards Parade is one of the best places for a grandstand view of the Queen's carriage as it heads up Whitehall for the State Opening of Parliament. We move on to the Strand, once one of the most influential thoroughfares in Britain, with many fine mansions, including the magnificent Somerset House, which has awesome grounds for central London.

The street names from here on give a clue to the past inhabitants. Think of dukes and earls – Arundel, Surrey and Essex – as the Strand enters Aldwych (a name that derives from 'Old Wic' meaning old settlement). The grand buildings in this area are symbols of the architectural legacy of the Empire. Where the Strand ends and Fleet Street begins are a number of banks. These serviced those working at the Inns of Court, including Lloyds Bank with its floral tiles, and Child & Co Bankers whch has one of the first cheques – made out in 1705.

The walk ends near another church, St Bartholomew-the-Great, which dates from 1123 and is still surrounded by small streets as it was in the Middle Ages. This is Smithfield, the scene of jousting, tournaments and fairs and the site for executions. During the Peasant's Revolt of 1381 the rebel leader Wat Tyler was stabbed by the Lord Mayorh and taken to St Bartholomew's Hospital, but soldiers dragged him out and decapitated him.

Looking across Parliament Square past national flags to the Houses of Parliament and Big Ben

the walk

1 Leave Westminster tube by Exit 3, following signs to the **Houses of Parliament**. Turn into Parliament Square to cross Margaret Street to **Westminster Abbey** and the adjacent St Margaret's Church. Return across Margaret Street to pass Parliament's vehicle entrance again and continue ahead as the road becomes Parliament Street, and then Whitehall. Follow it past the **Cenotaph**, a simple block of Portland Stone that commemorates those people who died in the two world wars, all the way to **Trafalgar Square**.

2 Cross the end of Northumberland Avenue to continue along the **Strand**, the road that links Westminster with the City of London. Turn right at Savoy Street, to see the **Queen's Chapel of the Savoy**; otherwise carry on along the Strand, past **Somerset House**.

3 Turn right into Surrey Street, past the **Roman Bath**, left into Temple Place and left again along Arundel Street. Go right at the Strand. The two churches in the middle of the road are St Mary-le-Strand and St Clement Danes. After these the road becomes **Fleet Street**.

4 After the banks of Lloyds and Child & Co turn right into **Whitefriars Street**. At the crossroads turn left and left again into Dorset Rise. Go right into St Bride's Avenue to pass **St Bride's Church** and reach Bride Lane. Turn left and right to **Ludgate Circus**.

5 Continue ahead up Ludgate Hill. Turn left into the street called Old Bailey and carry on to the **Central Criminal Court**, known as 'The Old Bailey' – it lies on the site of the notorious former Newgate Prison. Cross Newgate Street and follow Giltspur Street to reach **St Bartholomew's Hospital**.

6 Walk under the **archway** to the hospital, with the only remaining sculpture of Henry VIII, to visit St Bartholomew-the-Less, the parish church of the hospital where the Stuart architect Inigo Jones was baptised. As you continue past the central square

Nelson's Column and the fountain in Trafalgar Sqaure

MAP: AA Street by Street London
START: Westminster tube station
FINISH: Farringdon tube station
PATHS: paved streets
LANDSCAPE: streets and alleyways
PUBLIC TOILETS: Westminster Square and Smithfield
TOURIST INFORMATION: London, tel 020 7971 0027
THE PUB: The Bishop's Finger, 9 West Smithfield, EC1, closed Sat and Sun

Getting to the start

Westminster tube station is on the Circle and District lines. Westminster is in the congestion charge area and parking is severely limited, but you could try Great College Street underground car park.

Researched and written by:
Leigh Hatts, Deborah King

opposite Smithfield Market, notice the marks on the stone wall left by a Zeppelin raid during World War One. At **St Bartholomew-the-Great** bear left to go into Grand Avenue, running through the market building.

7 Cross Charterhouse Street to enter St John Street and then bear left into St John's Lane. A few paces further on you will find **St John's Gate**. Keep going to cross Clerkenwell Road, pass Grand Priory Church and enter narrow Jerusalem Passage. Turn left at the end, into Aylesbury Street, and follow the pavement through Clerkenwell Green and back to Clerkenwell Road. Cross

the main road and walk along Britton Street, turning right by a park down Benjamin Street. Go left and right to reach **Farringdon tube station** where the walk ends.

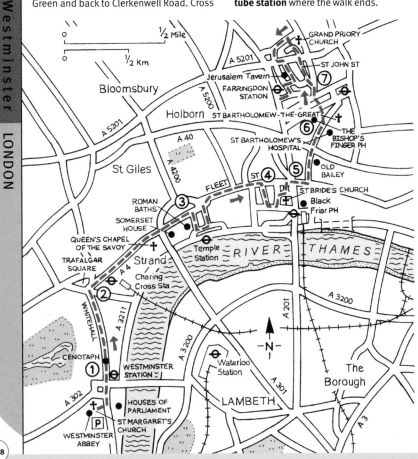

The Bishop's Finger

This smartly civilised pub, an outpost of Faversham's Shepherd Neame brewery, is one of the few places in London where you'll find their full complement of ales. Quietly tucked away in a little square beside Smithfield Market, it has a single, comfortable bar with polished bare boards, chunky, elegant wooden furnishings, large windows and pictures of old Smithfield adorning the walls. The open kitchen by the bar prepares some good lunchtime pub food. There's also an upstairs dining room, decent wines by the glass and friendly service.

about the pub

The Bishop's Finger
9 West Smithfield
London EC1A 9JR
Tel: 020 7248 2341

DIRECTIONS: West Smithfield; opposite St Bartholomews Hospital. Nearest tube: Farringdon	
PARKING: Smithfield is in the congestion charge area and parking is severely limited.	
OPEN: all day; closed Saturday and Sunday	
FOOD: daily	
BREWERY/COMPANY: Shepherd Neame	
REAL ALE: Shepherd Neame Bishop's Finger, Spitfire and seasonal ales	
DOGS: no dogs inside	

Food
Meat from Smithfield features heavily on the menu and includes a choice of 13 different sausages. Also available are ciabatta sandwiches and, on Thursday and Friday, beer-battered cod and chips.

Family facilities
Children are welcome at lunchtime.

Alternative refreshment stops
Try the Punch Tavern at Ludgate Circus (on walk, see Point 4).

☞ Where to go from here
While Westminster Abbey may seem like a tourist trap with its admission charge, if you go early in the morning before the coaches arrive, you can easily spend two or three hours here. Head towards the Barbican to find the Museum of London (150 London Wall), which illustrates over 2,000 years of London's history through imaginative reconstructions (www.museumoflondon.org.uk). Just off The Strand, in Covent Garden, is London's

Transport Museum (www.ltmuseum.co.uk), with its fantastic collection of road and rail vehicles, plus hands-on working exhibits, informative displays and interactive KidZones for children.

South Bank and Embankment

A walk along the South Bank, following its bridges.

The bridges of the River Thames

Westminster may have been the bridge that opened up the South Bank, but it was far from being a smooth operation. Initially built from stone in the 1740s, its opening was delayed by sabotage from ferrymen and the death of its sponsor. The Gothic patterns seen on the decorative wrought-iron bridge today are the work of Charles Barry when the bridge was rebuilt in 1853. Hungerford, the only combined rail and foot crossing, was built as a suspension bridge and bought in 1859 to extend the railway line to Charing Cross station.

When work began to replace the original Waterloo Bridge in 1939, World War Two was looming. The new bridge opened six years later, having been built mainly by women. Its architect, Sir Giles Gilbert Scott, was the man behind the Bankside power station, now the impressive Tate Modern

Another building with power station roots is the Oxo Wharf, which was acquired in the 1920s by thecompany that made Oxo cubes.

The present Blackfriars has five cast-iron arches. The remains of the rail bridge that once ran parallel look almost surreal, like the posts of a cochineal-tinted wedding cake rising out of the water.

The Millennium Bridge is the latest crossing, having officially opened in 2000. Southwark Bridge is the second on the site and beyond Cannon Street's railway bridge there is London Bridge, which has been renewed many times leaving us with the 20th-century version.

the walk

1 Leave Westminster tube station by Exit 1, following signs to **Westminster Pier**. Walk up the steps to your right and cross **Westminster Bridge**. Turn left along the riverfront. Ahead are the 32 transparent pods of the 2,100-ton (2,133-tonne) **London Eye**, a huge modern Ferris wheel. Just past Jubilee Gardens, on the right, is the next bridge, **Hungerford**.

2 Continue ahead past the **Royal Festival Hall** and look to the opposite bank of

Left: British Airways London Eye at South Bank
Right: Millennium Bridge

the Thames for a glimpse of Cleopatra's Needle. Beyond the Hayward Gallery and under **Waterloo Bridge** is the National Film Theatre and its outdoor café.

3 The path bends to the right, after the **Royal National Theatre**, before reaching the craft shops and restaurants of Gabriel's Wharf. Turn right at the Riviera restaurant and walk through the centre, lined on either side with small shops. Turn left at the end into **Upper Ground** and 100yds (91m) further on take another left turn into **Barge House Street**.

4 Ahead, an archway leads to the back of **Oxo Tower Wharf**. Enter the glass doors in the middle to catch the lift to the eighth floor for a better view of the skyline, or continue along the ground floor to the riverside exit.

5 Pass under **Blackfrairs Bridges**. The awesome ex-power station on your right was made with 4 million bricks. It is now home to one of the world's most popular art galleries, **Tate Modern**. If this is the only stop you make it will undoubtedly be a worthwhile one.

6 Continue past the **Millennium Foot Bridge** and **Shakespeare's Globe**. Beyond this is Southwark Bridge and, 200yds (183m) further on, Cannon Street Rail Bridge. A few paces on and you will pass the **Clink Museum**, on the site of the notorious old prison and the remnants of the Bishops' Palace – sadly just a 14th-century rose window and very little else. Ahead is a full-sized replica of Sir Francis Drake's 16th-century ship, the **Golden**

2h30	4.5 MILES	7.2 KM	LEVEL 1 2 3

MAP: OS Explorer 173 London North
START/FINISH: Westminster Station; grid ref: TQ 302796
PATHS: paved streets and riverside walk
LANDSCAPE: water and cityscape
PUBLIC TOILETS: South Bank Centre and on Embankment near Blackfriars Bridge
TOURIST INFORMATION: London, tel 020 7971 0027
THE PUB: The Anchor, Bankside, SE1
🚫 Keep children well supervised as this is a riverside walk

Getting to the start

Westminster tube station is on the Circle and District lines. Westminster is in the congestion charge area and parking is severely limited, but you could try Great College Street underground car park.

Researched and written by:
Leigh Hatts, Deborah King

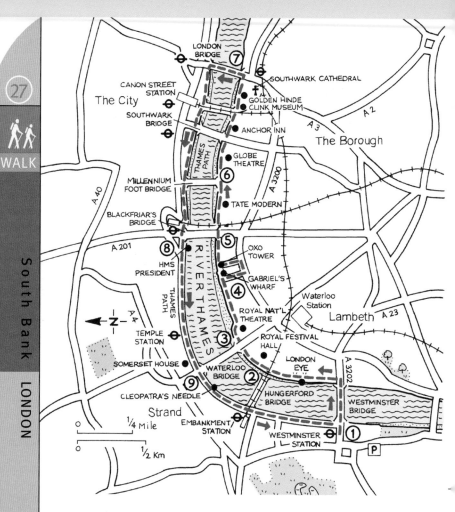

Hinde. Round the corner is Southwark Cathedral which was founded in 1106.

7 Cross **London Bridge** and descend the steps on the far side, following signs for the Thames Path (West).

8 At Blackfriars Bridge the Thames Path joins the wide pavement adjacent to the river. The first boat you will pass on your left is the HMS *President*. The next set of buildings to your right after Temple tube station belong to the **University of London**.

Further along you'll find majestic **Somerset House**.

9 A further 200yds (183m) ahead the path passes **Cleopatra's Needle** before reaching Embankment Station. Northumberland Avenue is the next road on your right. About 200yds (183m) further on is **Horse Guards Avenue**, sandwiched between the buildings of the Old War Office and the Ministry of Defence. When you reach Westminster Bridge turn right into Bridge Stree, to **Westminster tube station**.

The Anchor

In the shadow of the Globe Theatre, this historic pub lies on one of London's most famous tourist trails. Samuel Pepys supposedly watched the Great Fire of London from here in 1666, and Dr Johnson was a regular, with Oliver Goldsmith, David Garrick and Sir Joshua Reynolds. Although the original Anchor burnt down after the Great Fire, the present Georgian building that replaced it is atmospheric, with a rambling interior that has a maze of tiny rooms on several levels, intimate corners, old black beams, faded plasterwork and darkwood panelling. There's a large waterside terrace and the river views are excellent.

Food

The varied menu includes fish and chips, pan-fried halibut with olives, home-made pies and cod in crispy bacon, served on wilted spinach.

Family facilities

Children are not allowed on the ground floor, but may eat upstairs or on the patio.

Alternative refreshment stops

The Founders Arms is on Bankside near Tate Modern, or try the Refectory in Southwark Cathedral.

about the pub

The Anchor
34 Park Street, Bankside
London SE1 9EF
Tel: 020 7407 1577

DIRECTIONS: beside the Thames between Southwark Bridge and London Bridge.
Nearest tube/rail: London Bridge
PARKING: limited street parking
OPEN: daily; all day
FOOD: daily; all day
BREWERY/COMPANY: Spirit Group
REAL ALE: Wadworth 6X, Greene King IPA, guest beers
DOGS: not allowed inside

☛ Where to go from here

There's much to see and do on this walk. You'll pass the Hayward Gallery (www.hayward.org.uk). the Tate Modern (www.tate.org.uk), Shakespeare's Globe Exhibition and Tour (www.shakespeares-globe.org), the Clink Museum and the *Golden Hinde*. If you have the time (and are prepared to queue), take a trip on the London Eye (www.ba-londoneye.com) and view your walk and 55 of London's famous landmarks from high above the Thames. London Frogtours is a novel, 80-minute experience in a bright yellow amphibious craft that splashes down into the river at the Albert Embankment. Turn right at the London Eye and walk for about 100yds (91m) into Belvedere Road for departures.

The Inns of Court

Soak up the atmosphere of these hidden valleys and squares that featured in many of Dickens' novels.

Dickens in legal London

The compact area highlighted here between Temple and Fleet Street is home to some fine buildings that survived the Great Fire of London. Not only that, but to walk through this great legal institution is to take a step back in time. Charles Dickens, who was a keen walker, was a frequent visitor to

the area and used it as the setting for some of his novels.

Dickens first saw the darker side of life when his father was imprisoned for debt. He went to work in a shoe-blacking factory and it was this experience that formed the basis of his views on the injustice of poverty and that broadened his scope and insight. At the age of 15 he spent a year as a solicitor's clerk in Gray's Inn. Later he mastered the art of shorthand and took a job as a reporter on the *Morning Herald* before producing a series of articles for monthly and weekly publications, writing

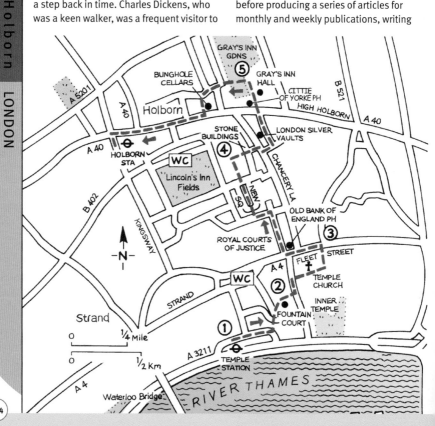

these under the pseudonym of 'Boz'. Dickens used these to highlight social issues and the plight of the poor. His novels were initially serialised, and Victorian readers, especially the lower middle classes, couldn't get enough of him – they would eagerly await the next instalment.

You'll see when you reach Fountain Court how little it can have changed in more than 150 years. The place is particularly atmospheric at dusk when the Victorian street lamps are alight. It is here that Tom meets his sister Ruth, in the novel *Martin Chuzzlewit* (1843). Further on, the Middle Temple, with its winding alleys and gardens, feels like a village. Based on his time as a solicitor's clerk, Dickens wrote: 'There is yet, in the Temple, something of a clerkly monkish atmosphere which public offices of law have not disturbed and even legal firms have failed to scare away...'

In *Martin Chuzzlewit*, Dickens describes how Tom felt about going to work in the Temple: '...he turned his face towards an atmosphere of unaccountable fascination, as surely as he turned it to the London smoke – until the time arrived for going home again and leaving it, like a motionless cloud behind'. Although the smoke is no longer around, you'll see what Dickens meant as you explore this calm little areaaway from the busy City streets.

the walk

1 Turn left at the exit to **Temple Station** and up a set of steps. Turn right into Temple Place. At the end go left into Milford Lane then, after a few more paces, go up another series of steps, into Essex Street. Turn right by the **Edgar Wallace pub** into

1h30 · **1.5 MILES** · **2.4 KM** · **LEVEL 123**

MAP: AA Street by Street london
START: Temple tube station
FINISH: Holborn tube station
PATHS: paved streets and alleyways
LANDSCAPE: alleyways and buildings of architectural interest
PUBLIC TOILETS: opposite the Law Courts in the Strand
TOURIST INFORMATION: City of London, tel 020 7332 1456
THE PUB: Cittie of Yorke, 22 High Holborn, WC1

Getting to the start
Temple tube station is alongside the Embankment on the Circle and District lines. Parking is severely limited.

Researched and written by:
Leigh Hatts, Deborah King

Holborn   LONDON

Devreux Court, walk through the gateway into The Temple and go down the steps to **Fountain Court**. (At weekends The Temple Inn of Court is often closed and you should go past the pub front to Fleet Street and turn right. Go left at the Old Bank of England to rejoin the route.)

2 Bear left under an archway into **Middle Temple**, past a small fountain and garden and up the steps, then bear right through some cloisters to reach the **Temple Church** (open for Sunday services). Go through an archway to the right of the church, then left through another archway and along a partly cobbled road to **Fleet Street**.

3 Turn left along Fleet Street and cross at the pedestrian lights. After the Old Bank of England pub turn right into **Bell Yard** and continue ahead on the path that runs alongside the **Royal Courts of Justice**. Turn left and then right into New Square and keep ahead.

4 Take the path on the far right along **Stone Buildings** and, ahead, go through the gates that lead to Chancery

Lane. Cross this road and turn right to go left into the street called Southampton Buildings. After just 20yds (18m) this veers sharply left, past the **London Silver Vaults**. Cross High Holborn and pass through a gateway to Gray's Inn on the right of the **Cittie of Yorke pub**. A few paces further, after Gray's Inn Hall, turn left into **Field Court**.

5 Continue to the end, then turn right and go up the steps into Jockeys Fields. Bear left along Bedford Row and take the second road on the left, **Hand Court**. Just past the Bunghole Cellars at the end, turn right along High Holborn to reach Holborn tube station.

what to look for

If you pop into the Old Bank of England pub, spare a thought for those whose lives were cut short. The vaults and tunnels below the Old Bank and the nearby buildings are where Sweeney Todd is reputed to have butchered clients, the remains of whom were served as fillings in the nearby pie shop of his mistress, Mrs Lovett.

Cittie of Yorke

A pub has stood on this site since 1430. In 1695, it was rebuilt as the Gray's Inn Coffee House and the large, low-vaulted cellar bar dates from this period. Easily identified from a distance by the large black-and-gold clock that hangs outside, it is a fine piece of Victorian architecture, deceptively large inside, with ornate ceilings and an impressive back room featuring a coal-burning stove dating back to the year of the Battle of Waterloo (1815), and intimate little booths across the very long bar. The gantry above is stacked with thousand-gallon wine vats. The panelled front bar features an original chandelier and portraits of illustrious locals, including Dickens and Sir Thomas More.

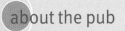
about the pub

Cittie of Yorke
22 High Holborn
London WC1
Tel: 020 7242 7670

DIRECTIONS: beside the gateway to Gray's Inn on High Holborn (on walk just before Point 5). Nearest tube: Chancery Lane	
PARKING: none	
OPEN: all day; closed Sunday	
FOOD: all day	
BREWERY/COMPANY: Samuel Smith Brewery	
REAL ALE: Old Brewery Bitter	
DOGS: not allowed inside	

Food
In addition to a variety of sandwiches, salads and soups, six hot dishes are freshly prepared each day, often including steak and ale pie and braised lamb shank.

Family facilities
Children are welcome in the eating area of the bar before 6pm.

Alternative refreshment stops
The Old Bank of England pub was a subsidiary branch of the Bank of England until the mid-1970s, when it became the flagship pub for Fuller's. It's a grand affair with chandeliers and high ceilings, and some surprisingly cosy corners. The Bunghole Cellars is a Davy's Wine Bar with sawdust on the floor, where ale is served by the half-gallon.

☞ Where to go from here
North of Holborn tube station, on Doughty Street near Russell Square tube, is the Charles Dickens Museum. The author lived in Doughty Street in his 20s and here you can see pages of his original manuscripts, together with valuable first editions and many personal mementoes (www.dickensmuseum.com). The Elizabethan Hall in the Middle Temple dates from the 16th century. It has a fine example of a double hammerbeam roof. Visitors are allowed in the hall and gallery from 10am to noon and from 3pm to 4pm.

Bargains in Borough

An urban walk south of the river to two of London's famous markets.

Borough, Bermondsey and Rotherhithe

Historically, Borough, Bermondsey and Rotherhithe were quite poor areas. Until a few years ago, nobody really wanted to live in Rotherhithe, but since the addition of new transport links, it has been attracting interest. To experience the specialist food and antiques markets here you will have to start this walk early – but you will be rewarded.

In the past, writers have been less than flattering about Rotherhithe, or Redriff as it was called when Samuel Pepys was writing his diaries. In *Our Mutual Friend* (1864–5), Charles Dickens writes of Rotherhithe, '...down by where accumulated scum of humanity seems to be washed from higher grounds like so much moral sewage...'. The early part of Moll Flander's career as a prostitute, according to the author Daniel Defoe, was also spent in Redriff. As in Docklands, developers have now created some expensive properties for those after a spot of lofty living, but the skyline was very different 200 years ago. Southwark Park now stands on the site of some of old market gardens. Although the area has more than its fair share of social housing, the markets have a richness unique to south London and the East End.

Borough Market is the last remaining early morning wholesale fruit and vegetable market in central London. Expect to see stalls selling anything from French cheeses and Cumbrian wild boar meat to barbecued burgers and organic vegetables. Enter from Stoney Street and witness the scene beneath the Victorian, cast-iron canopy.

Bermondsey Antiques Market operates on Fridays and is altogether different: the serious dealers have usually completed their trading by 4am. There are plenty of warehouses selling paintings, china, furniture and jewellery.

the walk

1 From Borough tube station turn left to cross Marshalsea Road and continue along **Borough High Street**, ignoring the left-hand slip road. A few paces past London Bridge tube station is **Borough Market**. Just after Bedale Street cross the road into St Thomas Street.

2 Take the first right into Weston Street, which runs past **Guy's Hospital's Greenwood Theatre** and the Rose pub on the corner of Snowsfields. Continue past the Bermondsey Leather Market building to Long Lane.

3 Turn left and follow Long Lane until you reach the junction with Bermondsey Street. On the right is the site of the open-air **Bermondsey Antiques Market**. Carry on ahead to cross Tower Bridge Road and enter Abbey Street. Turn right into **The Grange**. At the end turn left into Grange Road, then first left into Spa Road.

4 Just before the railway arch turn right into Rouel Road and then left into Dockley Road to go under the railway arch. At the end turn right into **St James's Road**, cross the road and take the path on the left, William Ellis Way, through some wooden posts.

Olives and oil for sale at Borough Market

3h00 — **5.5 MILES** — **8.8 KM** — **LEVEL 1 2 3**

WALK

5 Turn right to a T-junction and go left into Clements Road. At the end cross **Southwark Park Road**, using the pedestrian crossing, and turn right. Just beyond the Stanley Arms turn left into Southwark Park. Turn right and follow the path as it continues straight ahead before gently swinging to the left; the exit is before the **sports complex**. Turn left along Hawkstone Road to **Surrey Quays tube station**.

6 After crossing at the lights take Lower Road behind the station and in a short while go left into **Redriff Road**, beside the shopping complex.

7 Just before the bridge go right across the end of the redundant red lifting bridge and down steps to **Greenland Dock**. At the bottom of the steps bear left, past a long row of town houses facing Greenland Dock. Turn left after the bust of James Walker and, ignoring the first path, turn left under a bridge. At the top of the slope go left to follow a long straight path. Where the way divides keep ahead along the **old dockside paving**.

MAP: OS Explorer 173 London North
START: Borough tube station; grid ref: TQ 323797
FINISH: Rotherhithe tube station; grid ref: TQ 352979
PATHS: mainly paved
LANDSCAPE: historic streets, park and water
PUBLIC TOILETS: Southwark Park
TOURIST INFORMATION: Southwark, tel 020 7357 9168
THE PUB: The George, Southwark, SE1

Getting to the start
Borough is the heart of historic Southwark at the southern end of London Bridge. This is in the congestion charge area and there are no parking facilities. Borough tube station is on the Northern Line.

Researched and written by:
Leigh Hatts, Deborah King

Mouthwatering cheeses on sale at the Organic Market

Borough LONDON

WALK

8 At a junction go right and at once left to follow a curving path, ignoring a right turning, to the bottom of **Stave Hill**. Turn right to reach the Stave Hill steps. Here turn right and follow Dock Hill Avenue. Keep to the right of **Surrey Water** to reach Salter Road. Turn left along this main road, which leads into **Brunel Road**. Rotherhithe tube station is on the right.

what to look for

At the beginning of Redriff Road is a dockers' shelter. It was a hard life, for dockers were casual labourers who had to wait under this black awning each morning in the hope of being chosen for work. The number of men needed depended upon how many ships there were to unload.

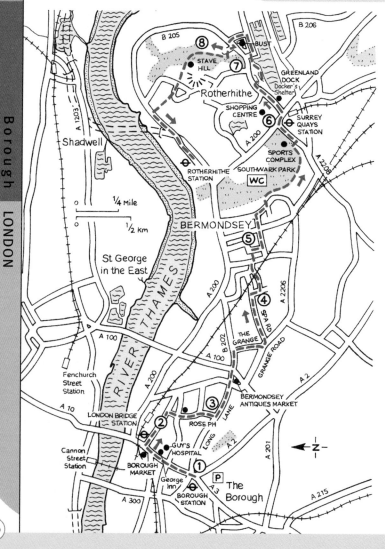

The George

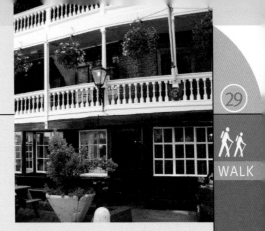

The only remaining galleried inn in London, this striking black-and-white building dates back at least to 1542, when it numbered one William Shakespeare among its clientele. It was rescued by the National Trust in the 1930s, and is certainly one of the capital's most celebrated landmarks. Dickens mentioned it in Little Dorrit, and his original life assurance policy is displayed along with 18th-century rat traps in the series of interlinked bars. The George Bar has low ceilings, dark beams, latticed windows and lantern lamps, and the Old Bar has a dark, quiet atmosphere and an open fireplace. This is a real old English pub with plenty of buzz.

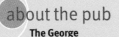

about the pub

The George
77 Borough High Street,
Southwark, London SE1 1NH
Tel: 020 7407 2056
www.georgeinn-southwark.co.uk

DIRECTIONS: on the right-hand side of Borough High Street just before Borough Market. (on walk shortly after Point 1).
Nearest tube: London Bridge

PARKING: none

OPEN: daily; all day

FOOD: no food Sunday evening

BREWERY/COMPANY: Greene King

REAL ALE: Fuller's London Pride and Greene King Abbot Ale

DOGS: no dogs inside

Food
The straightforward choice includes sandwiches, baguettes, steak and ale pie, traditional fish and chips, and sausage and mash, along with some decent real ales.

Family facilities
Children are welcome inside. Smaller portions of main dishes on the menu are available and there's plenty of al fresco seating on the large cobbled courtyard terrace overlooking the beautiful black-and-white frontage.

Alternative refreshment stops
Try the Stanley Arms in Southwark Park Road.

☞ Where to go from here
Climb the 60 steps up to the top of Stave Hill for a panoramic view of London, including the London Eye. A visit to the London Dungeon in Tooley Street will allow you to journey back to 1666 and relive the Great Fire of London, see the Torture Chamber, the Jack the Ripper Experience and wander through Victorian Whitechapel (www.thedungeons.com). A tour of HMS Belfast, Europe's last surviving big gun armoured warship from World War Two, will take you from the captain's bridge through nine decks to the massive boiler and engine rooms (www.iwm.org.uk/belfast).

Borough LONDON

The route of the Great Fire of London

A linear walk tracing the route of the great fire of 1666, an event that created a demand for new furniture.

The Great Fire

Londoners in the 17th century must have wondered what had hit them when, within months of fighting off the Great Plague, a fire of monumental proportions began at a bakery in Pudding Lane. It was 2AM on September 1666 when the baker discovered the fire. Although 13,000 houses, 87 churches and 40 livery halls perished in the flames, Incredibly, only eight people lost their lives, although how many later died after being left homeless is unknown. It took five days to contain the fire, partly because of the high number of houses with timber roofs and the rudimentary fire-fighting equipment available at the time.

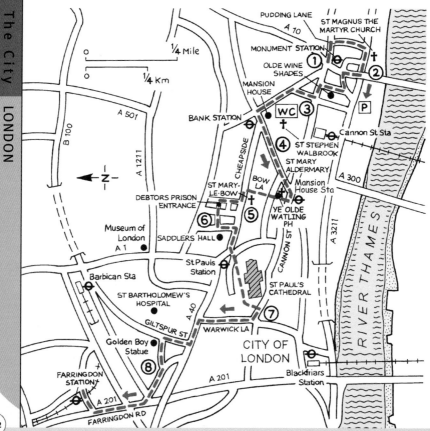

The event offered an opportunity to give the city a facelift, but due to the sheer cost and to property rights most of the rebuilding followed the original street lines. It did, however, create a safer, more sanitary capital than before, and with the new houses came a demand for furniture.

Within six years the city had been rebuilt, extended and London was in the middle of an economic boom. By 1700 the population had increased five-fold to 500,000 inhabitants and the city's manufacture of chests and cabinets led the way. Perhaps the most common item produced by a cabinet-maker were table, candlestands and mirror ensembles, which were a standard item in many homes. Cabinets were made by skilled craftsmen and therefore more expensive. However, the same techniques were later used for chests of drawers.

Brisk trade with North America, the East Indies, East India and the Far East introduced new styles such as lacquerware. Cane chairs were also introduced from the Far East and most middle-class homes had one or more of these 'English chairs'. With the demand for furniture of all types and to match all pockets, the life of a tradesman in the late 1600s was a happy one indeed.

the walk

1 Take the **Fish Street Hill exit** from Monument tube station and turn right towards the **Monument**. (For a detour follow the cobbled street behind the Monument to see the plaque that marks the spot on the corner of Pudding Lane where the ill-fated bakery once stood.) Continue downhill and cross Lower Thames Street at the

| 2h00 | 2.25 MILES | 3.6 KM | LEVEL 1 2 3 |

WALK

MAP: AA Street by Street London
START: Monument tube station
FINISH: Farringdon tube station
PATHS: paved streets
LANDSCAPE: alleyways and City roads
PUBLIC TOILETS: Monument and Mansion House
TOURIST INFORMATION: City of London, tel 020 7332 1456
THE PUB: Ye Olde Watling, 29 Watling Street, EC4, closed Sat and Sun

Getting to the start

Monument tube station is in Eastcheap at the north end of London Bridge and in the congestion charge area. There is no parking. The station is on the District and Circle lines.

Researched and written by:
Leigh Hatts, Deborah King

The City

WALK

The City

pedestrian crossing to reach **St Magnus the Martyr Church**.

2 A few paces further to the right of the church, climb a set of steps and, ignoring the first exit, walk on to arrive on the west side of London Bridge. Continue ahead, away from the river, along King William Street and shortly turn left along Arthur Street and then sharp right into Martin Lane, past the **Olde Wine Shades**. At the end turn left into Cannon Street.

3 Cross the road and turn right into **Abchurch Lane**. At the end bear left along King William Street towards Bank tube station. Keep to the left, past the front of **Mansion House**, and notice the street on the left, Walbrook: this is the site of one of Wren's finest churches, St Stephen Walbrook.

The church of St Mary-le-Bow

what to look for

The statue of the 'Golden Boy' on the building at the corner of Cock Lane marks the spot where the fire is thought to have ended. On this site, until 1910, stood a pub called The Fortune of War, where body-snatchers would leave bodies on benches and wait to hear from the surgeons of the nearby St Bartholomew's Hospital.

4 Continue ahead, along Queen Victoria Street, then turn right into Bow Lane, past St Mary Aldermary, **Ye Olde Watling pub** and a row of shops, to St Mary-le-Bow at the end. Turn left into **Cheapside** which, despite being the widest road in the City, also went up in flames.

5 Cross this road, turn right into Milk Street and take the narrow alley on the right, **Mitre Court**. Follow it round to enter a courtyard with an eerie entrance to the **old debtors' prison**. Carry on through the alley, to the left of the Hole in the Wall pub, to Wood Street.

6 Cross the road into Goldsmith Street and, at the **Saddlers Hall** opposite, turn left and rejoin Cheapside. Turn right and go over the pedestrian crossing to **St Paul's Cathedral**. Follow the churchyard railing on the left to reach the cathedral front at the top of Ludgate Hill.

7 Turn right at Mark's & Spencer into Ave Maria Lane, which becomes Warwick Lane. At the end turn left along **Newgate Street**. At the traffic lights turn right along Giltspur Street, then left into Cock Lane.

8 At a junction turn right down Snow Hill to Farringdon Road. Go right to reach **Farringdon tube station** where the walk ends.

Ye Olde Watling

The pub was built in 1604 to house the workers on St Paul's and stands on London's oldest street, overlooking the great cathedral from its doorway. Today, the beamed and panelled ground-floor bar with its leaded windows and bright copper jugs is a favourite rendezvous for after-office drinkers. The upstairs bar, Wren's Room, has chintzy Victorian charm, while at the rear is a small games room offering darts and pool.

Food

There's a good traditional menu featuring sandwiches, fish and chips and steak and kidney pie.

Family facilities

Children are welcome in the upstairs restaurant. On fine days retreat to the sheltered rear courtyard, which has picnic benches.

Alternative refreshment stops

The Place Below, a vegetarian restaurant in the crypt of St Mary-le-Bow Church, offers discounts to those who arrive before midday.

☛ Where to go from here

Head for the Museum of London in nearby London Wall to find out more about the Great Fire and the devastation witnessed by Samuel Pepys. This is the world's largest urban history museum – it offers an insight into London life from the Roman era to the 18th century. Many artefacts are on display, including a tiny crucifix delicately carved from bone by an inmate of Newgate Prison (www.museumoflondon.org.uk). Allow time to visit St Paul's Cathedral to see the carvings of Grinling Gibbons, the Whispering Gallery and the Crypt with many famous tombs (www.stpauls.co.uk).

about the pub

Ye Olde Watling
29 Watling Street
London EC4M 9BR
Tel: 020 7653 9971

DIRECTIONS: the pub is in narrow Bow Lane (on walk just after Point 4). Nearest tube: Mansion House	
PARKING: none	
OPEN: all day; closed Saturday and Sunday	
FOOD: all day	
BREWERY/COMPANY: Mitchells & Butlers	
REAL ALE: Adnams Bitter, Fuller's London Pride	
DOGS: not allowed inside	

The City LONDON

Old and new Docklands

Wandering through the Docklands, home to the world's oldest police force.

Docklands and pioneer Police

Docklands has evolved from being one of the busiest ports in the world to being one of the most expensive dock developments. Yet there is a stillness to the area, as if the Victorian warehouses have not quite come to terms with their modern neighbours, of which the striking Canary Wharf complex is surely the best example.

The police station in Wapping High Street, not open to the public, is identified by the sign 'Metropolitan Police Marine Support', as the men and women here are responsible for policing the Thames.

In the 18th century many thousands of men worked in the docks handling imports that included fine cloth, precious metals and spices. Petty thefts were commonplace and around 100 pirates operated between London Bridge and Gravesend alone. John Harriott, a Justice of the Peace, and Patrick Colquhoun, a magistrate – decided to do something about it. In 1798 they obtained approval from Parliament to finance the first preventative policing of the river . It was a resounding success: within six months the Marine Police had saved an astounding £112,000 worth of cargo. But it wasn't until 1878, when the Princess Alice paddle steamer sank near Barking with the loss of over 600 lives, that the rowing galleys the Marine Police had been using were replaced with more powerful craft. Today the teams use Rigid Inflatable Boats (RIBs) and larger, more conventional vessels.

the walk

1 Take the underpass from Tower Hill Station that leads to the **Tower of London**. In front of the moat are the remains of the east gate of the medieval wall that once surrounded the City. Turn right and follow the lower path round the **moat** to go through the main gates to the Tower of London and follow the cobbled path for 440yds (402m).

2 Cross the road and enter **St Katharine Dock**. After a short distance turn left to pass Starbucks, cross a footbridge, follow a line of shops and walk over the Telford Footbridge. Go left to take the path at the side of the **Dickens Inn**. Pass along the back of the pub and turn left into Mews Street. On reaching water again go right with Mews Street.

3 Turn right into Thomas More Street. At a junction keep right with Thomas More Street to meet **Wapping High Street**. Turn left along this street of wharfs, luxury developments and Victorian warehouses.

Boats in St Katherine's Dock at London's Docklands

31

| 1h45 | 3.5 MILES | 5.7 KM | LEVEL 123 |

WALK

MAP: OS Explorer 173 London North

START: Tower Hill tube station; grid ref: TQ 335807

FINISH: Canary Wharf DLR station; grid ref: TQ 364803

PATHS: paved streets and riverside paths

LANDSCAPE: river and dramatic new Docklands buildings

PUBLIC TOILETS: Tower Hill and Canary Wharf

TOURIST INFORMATION: Tower Hamlets, tel 020 7375 2539

THE PUB: Prospect of Whitby, 59 Wapping Wall, E1

🛈 This is a riverside walk, so children should be well supervised

The blue-and-white 1970s-style building on your right is the **Metropolitan Police boatyard**. Carry on past Il Bordello restaurant and the police station.

4 Continue ahead past Wapping Lane and Wapping Station. After the road bends to the left at **New Crane Wharf**, turn right into Wapping Wall, signposted 'Thames Path'. Just past the **Prospect of Whitby** pub cross a bridge over Shadwell Basin.

5 Turn right with the Thames Path alongside the sports ground to enter the **Edward VII Memorial Park** where there is a superb view of Canary Wharf. After a blue apartment block the path bends away from the river and joins Narrow Street; it later crosses the **Limehouse Basin** and passes the Grapes pub.

6 Turn right into Three Colt Street and walk to the end, where you meet the river again at the **Canary Riverside path**. Continue ahead to Canary Wharf Pier.

The Tower of London's White Tower is an 11th-century hall keep with capped turrets

Getting to the start

Tower Hill is at the east end of The City just behind the Tower of London. Tower Hill tube station is on the Circle and District lines. This is in the congestion charge area and there are no parking facilities. Try Lower Thames Street car park.

Researched and written by:
Leigh Hatts, Deborah King

7 Walk up the steps on the left of the pier, cross the road to **Westferry Circus** and continue in the direction of Canary Wharf, which is immediately ahead. Follow West India Avenue into **Cabot Square** to enter the shopping centre where there is the **Canary Wharf DLR station** entrance.

what to look for

Rising to 800ft (244m), the Canary Wharf Tower is the flagship of the Canary Wharf development, so named because, when the site was used as a dock, many of the imports were from the Canary Islands. The tower has 50 floors and nearly 4,000 windows.

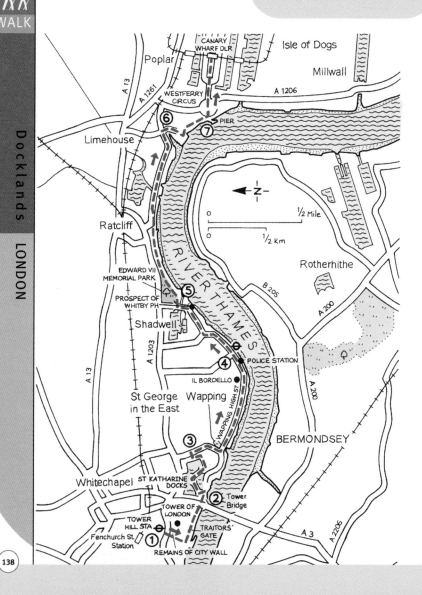

The Prospect of Whitby

about the pub

Prospect of Whitby
59 Wapping Wall
London E1W 3SH
Tel: 020 7481 1095

DIRECTIONS: beside the Thames at Shadwell Basin. Nearest tube: Wapping (on the walk just before Point **5**)	
PARKING: roadside parking	
OPEN: daily; all day	
FOOD: daily; all day	
BREWERY/COMPANY: Spirit Group	
REAL ALE: Fuller's London Pride, Greene King Old Speckled Hen	
DOGS: welcome throughout the pub	

Originally known as The Devil's Tavern, this famous 16th-century inn has been a meeting place for sailors and was also a gruesome setting for public executions. Samuel Pepys was a regular here before the tavern was remodelled and renamed in 1777. Charles Dickens and the notorious 'Hanging Judge' Jeffreys also drank here, and the artist J M W Turner spent time here studying the river views. Today, old ships timbers retain the seafaring traditions of this venerable riverside inn, which also has flagged floors, low ceilings, old fireplaces, pebbled windows and a rare pewter bar counter resting on old wooden casks. There's also a splendid terrace overlooking the Thames for summer alfresco drinking.

Food
Popular dishes include beef Wellington, minted lamb loins and a good selection of fish, alongside decent sandwiches, ploughman's lunches and filled jacket potatoes.

Family facilities
Children of all ages are welcome inside. Although there is no children's menu, smaller portions can be provided and there are high chairs for younger family members.

Alternative refreshment stops
The Dickens Inn in St Katharine Dock, the Grapes in Narrow Street or the cafés at Canary Wharf.

☛ Where to go from here
See the Crown Jewels, Traitors' Gate, the Royal Armouries and the famous ravens at the Tower of London (www.hrp.org.uk), one of London's most famous sights. Visit the Tower Bridge Exhibition within the two towers which brings to life the story of Tower Bridge, and take in magnificent panoramic views of London. Spread over five floors of a Georgian warehouse, the Museum in Docklands preserves the rich and varied history of London's river and port and tells the stories of people who lived and worked in the area (www.museumindocklands.org.uk).

From Waltham Abbey to Tottenham

Discover hidden wildlife and London's industrial history.

Waltham Abbey

Waltham was the last abbey in the country to be dissolved by Henry VIII in 1540. A settlement since Saxon times, Waltham came to prominence when Tovi the Proud, a member of King Canute's court, brought a stone crucifix (the Holy Rood or Holy Cross) from his estate in Somerset to the Lee Valley in the 11th century. According to legend the cross was supposed to be taken to Glastonbury Abbey (15 miles/24km from where it was discovered), but the oxen refused to go in that direction and instead travelled across the country until they reached Waltham. The town prospered from pilgrims flocking to the shrine of the Holy Rood. Waltham Abbey is also notable as the

burial place of King Harold II after his death at the Battle of Hastings in 1066. From the 1600s Waltham's gunpowder mills became the town's major employers. It is reputed that both the gunpowder used by Guy Fawkes and the explosives used in the Dam Busters raids were manufactured here.

the ride

1 From the pub head south along the gravel tow path past **Hazlemere Marina**, which has toilets and a café. Shortly before reaching the M25 you will see the Sea Scout base on **Rammey Island** to the left.

2 Rammey Marsh Lock is the first on this ride; Rammey Marsh is the open expanse to the right. On this section part of a **dismantled bridge** has been converted into a good vantage point. A 1998 bridge

Stone Bridge Lock

carries Ordnance Road over the navigation and tow path. The Greyhound pub is immediately to the south.

3 At **Enfield Lock** the path moves to the east bank. Take care crossing the road here on the sharp bend. You will soon reach the **Swan and Pike Pool,** once a place for bathing but now a picnic area. It takes its name from a pub that used to stand here. The tow path passes under a disused railway bridge. The high bank of **King George's Reservoir** soon looms on the left, marking the start of almost 4 miles (6.4km) of reservoirs. Look out for the **sculptures** on the right past the blue footbridge.

4 The double lock at **Ponders End** is preceded by the huge timber-framed bulk of the Navigation Inn. At the locks the path plunges under the bridge carrying Lea Valley Road, which runs between **King George's Reservoir** and William Girling Reservoir.

5 At the North Circular Road the tow path joins a concrete road alongside the **Lea Valley Trading Estate**. Take care on this section, which is shared with out-of-service buses heading to the Arriva garage. Past the bus depot the route goes under the footbridge and the path is once again traffic-free, wide and well surfaced.

6 The tow path returns to the west bank at **Stonebridge Lock** for the final run to Tottenham Lock. Those tired out by the southbound ride may wish to return north by train from Tottenham Hale to Waltham Cross, about a mile (1.6km) from the Old English Gentleman.

4h00 · **14 MILES** · **22.8 KM** · **LEVEL 1**23

CYCLE

Waltham Abbey

ESSEX

MAP: OS Explorer 174 Epping Forest & Lee Valley

START/FINISH: The Old English Gentleman, Waltham Abbey; grid ref: TL 375006

TRAILS/TRACKS: largely compacted gravel tow path, some tarmac and paved sections

LANDSCAPE: industrial and waterside

PUBLIC TOILETS: Hazlemere Marina, Waltham Abbey

TOURIST INFORMATION: Waltham Abbey, tel 01992 652295

CYCLE HIRE: Abbey Cross Discount Cycle Centre, Waltham Cross, tel 01992 651135

THE PUB: Old English Gentleman, Waltham Abbey, EN9

🛇 Some narrow gaps at locks. A free permit is necessary to cycle along the Lee Navigation – see www.waterscape.com

Getting to to the start

Waltham Abbey is just outside the M25 and is accessible from junction 26 via the A121. The Old English Gentleman is west of the town centre on the road to Waltham Cross. Please ask permission before parking at the pub. The alternative is to use the pay-and-display in Waltham Abbey town centre.

Why do this cycle ride?

This is a totally off-road ride from the north-eastern edge of Greater London to the urban bustle of Tottenham through the green corridor of the Lee Valley. It is also linear, so you can turn round at any time if you get tired.

Researched and written by: James Hatts

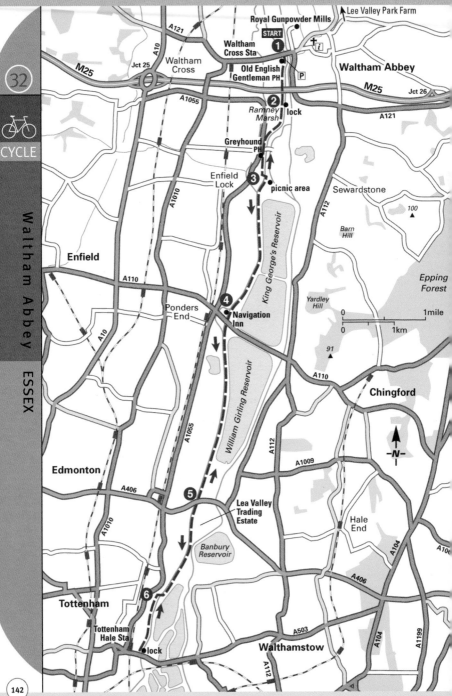

The Old English Gentleman

☞ **Where to go from here**
Visit the great Norman church and the remains of the abbey buildings at Waltham Abbey, just a few hundred yards from the start of the ride (www.walthamabbeychurch.co.uk). Also at Waltham Abbey are the Royal Gunpowder Mills, which are open every weekend during the summer (www.royalgunpowdermills.com). You can view many types of farm animals, including a variety of rare breeds in a traditional-style farmyard at Lee Valley Park Farm at Crooked Mile. Children will also enjoy the pet centre and summer tractor rides (www.leevalleypark.com).

This small, two-bar pub is just south of Waltham Lock and minutes away from the abbey church and the shops and facilities of Waltham Abbey. The cosy, compact interior is complemented by a large riverside terrace. The pub is run in a traditional way, with the emphasis on quality beer and good food, and holds regular real ale festivals and events. It's busy at weekends, but surprisingly quiet, even on sunny summer weekdays.

Food
Expect a modest menu of well-priced and well-presented dishes from fish and chips to lamb rogan josh, as well as lighter options such as jacket potatoes and a range of ploughman's meals.

Family facilities
Children are welcome inside and there's a small play area at the rear of the pub.

Alternative refreshment stops
There's a café at Hazlemere Marina and several waterside pubs along the Lee Navigation.

about the pub

Old English Gentleman
Highbridge Street,
Waltham Abbey
Essex EN9 1BA
Tel: 01992 713222

DIRECTIONS: see Getting to the start
PARKING: Ample parking is available for patrons at the pub. Others are welcome to park here, but please inform the landlord on arrival
OPEN: daily; all day
FOOD: daily; all day
BREWERY/COMPANY: free house
REAL ALE: Everard's Tiger, Tetley Imperial, Fuller's London Pride

From Bow to Walthamstow Marshes

Explore the Lee Navigation and East London's surprising open spaces.

Walthamstow Marshes

Walthamstow Marshes provide a haven for many types of wildlife not found elsewhere in Greater London. The marshland habitat sustains a breeding bird community including reed bunting, and reed, sedge and willow warblers. A variety of wintering birds visit the marshes and neighbouring reservoirs, and in autumn finches can be found feeding on the seeds of the tall herbs. Rare breed cattle, including longhorn, which have been reintroduced after an absence of more than 100 years, now graze the land. The cattle manage the vegetation, allowing creeping marshwort, which is only found at one other site, to thrive. Remains of pre-Viking boats have been found on the marshes, testimony to the early navigational importance of the

Lee. It was on Walthamstow Marshes that the first all-British powered flight was made by Alliott Verdon Roe in 1909. A blue plaque marks the railway arch where he assembled his triplane.

the ride

1 Start on the Tesco side of the bridge leading to **Three Mills Island** and look for the narrow entrance to the tow path heading north. Soon you reach a wide **quay**; head up the ramp just before the gas depot. Take care crossing the road under the Bow flyover. The path then crosses Bow Back River before returning to the tow path. At the railway bridge, the large building on the left is the **former Bryant & May match factory**. As you approach Old Ford Lock the Lee Navigation diverges from the course of the river; there is a very narrow gap for bicycles on the bridge which carries the path across the river. Rather than squeezing through the gap you may find it easier to use the stairs on the far side of the bridge where there is no such barrier.

2 At **Old Ford Lock** the former lockkeeper's house is well known as the home of Channel 4's cult 1990s morning show *The Big Breakfast*, and parts of the set can still be seen in the garden. Soon the junction with the **Hertford Union Canal** is reached. A series of road and railway bridges cross the Navigation in quick succession. Beyond the Homerton Road bridge the Navigation runs alongside **Hackney Marsh**, and the route for cyclists leaves the tow path to run on the inland side of the fence. Just past the **white gate** across the track return to the tow path.

3 A long brick wall marks the edge of the **Middlesex Filter Beds Nature Reserve**. At the bridge the tow path moves to the west bank. Past the Princess of Wales pub there is a rough section of path under the bridge. It then skirts the edge of **North Millfields Recreation Ground**. The navigation is bordered by housing to the west and **Walthamstow Marshes** to the east. Beyond the railway bridge and the Anchor and Hope pub is Springfield Park. The route heads inland to pass the **adventure playground**.

4 At the bottom of Spring Hill there is a useful waterside café. Cross the bridge here to reach **Springfield Marina,** and continue straight ahead with Warwick Reservoir on your left and the marina on your right. At the vehicle entrance to the marina, stay on the surfaced roadway; look for the painted **bicycle symbol**. Mind your head as you pass underneath the low railway bridge. Turn right immediately through the gate into the playing field. The undulating gravel track enjoys some excellent views.

5 Soon the track scoops down under the railway junction and emerges on to a wide causeway. The **Lea Bridge Riding School** is to the left. The left-hand tunnel under the Lea Bridge Road is for cyclists.

2h00	8.5 MILES	13.7 KM	LEVEL 1 2 3

MAP: OS Explorer 162 Greenwich & Gravesend and 173 Epping Forest and Lee Valley

START/FINISH: Three Mills, Bow; grid ref: SK 241515

TRAILS/TRACKS: mixed; some surfaced paths, some gravel tracks

LANDSCAPE: waterside, marsh and parkland

PUBLIC TOILETS: at Springfield Park

TOURIST INFORMATION: Greenwich, tel 0870 608 2000

CYCLE HIRE: none locally

THE PUB: The Kings Arms, Bow, E3

🛈 One major road crossing

Getting to the start

Three Mills Island can be reached via Hancock Road from the Bow Interchange where the A11 meets the A12 Blackwall Tunnel Northern Approach. Follow signs to Tesco Superstore, south of the A11/A118 interchange. You can use the Tesco car park.

Why do this cycle ride?

This is an enjoyable circuit linking many points of interest in the Lower Lee Valley. From the industrial history of Three Mills to 1990s television nostalgia and the first all-British powered flight, this ride has it all.

Researched and written by: James Hatts

Top: Three Mills
Left: Hackney Marshes

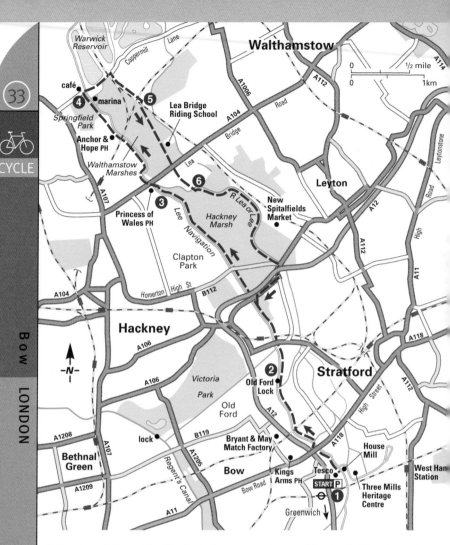

Warwick Reservoir
Coppermill Lane
Walthamstow
0   ½ mile
0   1km
café
④ marina **⑤**
Lea Bridge Riding School
Springfield Park
A1006
A104
Bridge
A112
Road
Anchor & Hope PH
Walthamstow Marshes
Lea
⑥
Leyton
New Spitalfields Market
Princess of Wales PH **③**
Lee Navigation
R Lea or Lee
A12
Leytonstone
A107
Hackney Marsh
Leyton Road
High
A11
Clapton Park
A104
Homerton High St
B112
Hackney
A106
A106
Victoria Park
Old Ford
② Old Ford Lock
Stratford
A112
A118
Bethnal Green
A1208
A107
lock
Regent's Canal
A1205
B119
Old Ford
A12
Bryant & May Match Factory
High Street
House Mill
West Ham Station
A1209
Bow
Kings Arms PH
Bow Road
Tesco
START 🅿
①
Three Mills Heritage Centre
Greenwich
−N−

Follow the path through the filter beds. A distinctive **red bridge** carries the path across the River Lee and on to Hackney Marsh.

⑥ Once across the bridge, turn left and follow the tree-lined **riverside path**. This section features a 'trim trail' of fitness equipment. There are views of the Temple Mills railway depot and New Spitalfields Market. At the bridge linking the marsh with the recreation ground across the river,

continue straight ahead. When the path emerges on to Homerton Road, use the toucan crossing. Pass under the flyover and turn right along **Eastway**, using the cycle lane on the pavement. Continue past the service station. Just before the bridge across the Navigation keep your eyes peeled for a **blue squeeze-gate**, which provides access to the tow path. On joining the tow path, turn left and return to **Three Mills** via the outward route.

The Kings Arms

about the pub

The Kings Arms
167 Bow Road, Bow
London E3 2SG
Tel: 020 8981 1398

DIRECTIONS: on the A11 close to Bow
Church. To reach it from Three Mills follow
the route to Bow Flyover, cross the road and
turn left up the hill past the church

PARKING: there is no parking close to
the pub

OPEN: daily; all day

FOOD: no food Saturday lunchtime and
Sunday evening

BREWERY/COMPANY: free house

REAL ALE: none served

*The Kings Arms is a traditional East End
pub and attracts a predominantly local
clientele. This is not the smartest or
most modern of pubs, but is ideal for
a reasonably priced Thai meal and a
drink before or after tackling your ride.
The historic church of St Mary's Bow –
sometimes known as Bow Church – is
on an island in the middle of the road
just across from the pub. There are
some seats on the wide pavement
outside. Cycle racks are also available
right outside the pub.*

Food

Thai cuisine is the culinary attraction.
Starters range from chicken wings in
garlic sauce to tofu surprise. Main courses
include curries and stir-fry dishes, and
there's deep-fried ice-cream for dessert.
On Sunday afternoons a traditional roast
lunch is served, with a limited selection
from the Thai menu available.

Family facilities

Although there are no special facilities for
children they are welcome inside the pub.

Alternative refreshment stops

Try the café at Springfield Marina or one
of the riverside pubs.

☛ Where to go from here

Three Mills Island boasts hundreds of years
of industrial heritage and the House Mill is
Britain's oldest and largest restored tidal
mill, built in 1776. Together with the Clock
Mill, re-built in 1817, they are two of the
most elegant waterside buildings in
London. You can tour the House Mill on
Sundays between May and September.
There are also trips on East London's canals
from here (www.leevalleypark.org.uk).

The waterways of the East End

Discover the history of the East End waterways on this tow path walk.

River Lea and Canals

In the mid-19th century the banks of the River Lea were lined with flourishing industries. At that time, because it was deemed to be outside the City of London with its stringent pollution regulations, the water and surrounding air quality were dangerously poor. Since the demise of canal transport, this area, has been transformed into a clean, peaceful haven for both walkers and wildlife.

As the Industrial Revolution progressed in the 19th century, the River Lea became an enormous health hazard. The factories along its banks produced a great deal of waste – the river was, in effect, used as a dumping ground for chemical and pharmaceutical waste. Looking at the scene before you today, it's not easy to picture a skyline of mass industrialism. Warehouses, cranes and gas works were here, against a backdrop of smoggy, smelly air. But, together with the noise of the powerful machinery, this would have been a way of life for many workers. For more than half of the 20th-century, barges still brought raw materials to the factories from London Docks, taking away the finished goods. Today, however, you're more likely to see a heron than a vessel on this stretch of the river.

the walk

1 From the end of Three Mill Lane, running between Tesco's supermarket car park, take the footpath to the left of an iron bridge leading to **Three Mills**. Continue walking with the river to your right-hand

2h30 — 4.25 MILES — 6.8 KM — LEVEL 123

side and you will shortly see the formidable volume of traffic coming into view, going across the **Bow Flyover**.

2 Where the path ends walk up the ramp on your left, leading to the A12. Turn right and cross the A11 ahead of you. Now walk down the slope and across a bridge to rejoin the tow path, with the river now to your left. Notice the brickwork of the old Bryant & May match factory ahead to your left. The path swings right, away from the traffic. Ignore the Greenway sign on the right and pass under two pipes that are part of the **old Victorian sewer**. Cross a bridge and continue along the River Lea, past the **Old Ford Lock**.

3 Just before the next bridge ahead, the **Hertford Union Canal** emerges and joins at a right angle on the left. Cross the bridge and turn left down a slope to join this canal along a gravel path. Pass Bottom Lock, Middle Lock and, further on, Top Lock. Once past the cottages of Top Lock, **Victoria Park** is visible on the right. Continue along this long, straight, paved path until you pass under **Three Colts Bridge** and two further bridges.

4 Cross a footbridge at a T-junction of the waterways to pick up the southern section of the **Regent's Canal**, which was opened in 1820 and used by horse-drawn barges to haul coal through London. (For **The Crown** pub, don't join the canal, instead divert right to the road and turn right to find the pub at the end of a terrace). Continue along the canal and soon the blinking light of **Canary Wharf** will be a landmark. Pass under a railway bridge, Mile

MAP: OS Explorer 162 Greenwich & Gravesend

START/FINISH: Three Mills; grid ref: TQ 383828

PATHS: good tow paths

LANDSCAPE: industrial waterside and park

PUBLIC TOILETS: none on route

TOURIST INFORMATION: Tower Hamlets, tel 020 7375 2539

THE PUB: The Crown, 223 Grove Road, E3
⚠ Care to be taken with children at all times as the route is beside water

Getting to the start

Three Mills is off the A12 between Bow and the Isle of Dogs. The nearest tube station is Bromley-by-Bow on the District Line. From the station turn left down steps to go under the road and on the far side go right again to walk down and bear right into Hancock Road, then go down Three Mill Lane by Tesco's Supermarket. There is also a car park in Three Mill Lane.

Researched and written by:
Leigh Hatts, Deborah King

End Lock, two more bridges and Jonson's Lock. Pass a **red brick chimney**, which is a sewer ventilation shaft, and walk under a railway bridge. Continue past **Salmon Lock** and notice the viaduct ahead. After walking under **Commercial Road Bridge**, turn left and follow the steps to the road.

5 Turn right along Commercial Road and pass **Limehouse Library** and a small park on the right. Pass over a bridge and take the steps on the right-hand side that lead down to the canal. Turn right and follow the tow path of the canal, the **Limehouse Cut**, with the water on your left. A few paces further on pass under the A13. Follow the path under three more bridges. Just before the A102 take the **boarded walkway** under the road.

what to look for

A Swedish manufacturer of matchsticks sold the British patent to Mr Bryant and Mr May who, in 1855, leased the factory, Bryant & May. A medical condition called 'phossy jaw' was common among workers and was often fatal. The fumes from the yellow phosphorous in the head of the match caused the jawbone to rot away – the smell from the diseased bone was apparently horrendous. In 1911 a new factory was built on the site and has now been converted into luxury flats.

6 At **Bow Locks** walk over the concrete footbridge and under two bridges. Continue ahead towards **Three Mills**. Turn left over the bridge back to the start.

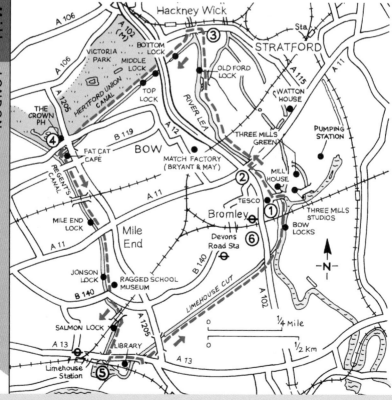

The Crown

The Crown is a beautifully restored, listed Victorian building spread over two floors, with pleasant views across South Hackney's Victoria Park. The open-plan bar with its boarded floors, old wood tables and comfy sofas is equally suited to lively conversation or peaceful newspaper reading on quiet afternoons (no music, electronic machines or TV). Upstairs, in a series of dining rooms with balconies, modern British cooking is presented on seasonal, twice-daily changing menus. Everything is totally organic, including the beer and wines – the Crown is the second officially certified organic pub in Britain.

Food
Good-value weekend breakfasts and brunch, a bargain weekday lunch, and a two-course dinner menu supplement the short à la carte menu, and all ingredients are strictly organic. Starters might include tagliatelle with lemon cream, parsley and parmesan, or asparagus and white bean minestrone, followed by polenta and gorgonzola fritters with cauliflower, pine nut and raisin salad, or roast venison fillet with beetroot bubble and squeak and red wine sauce.

Family facilities
Families are very welcome. Smaller portions of adult dishes are provided and there are high chairs and baby-changing facilities in the toilets, and seats and tables in the front garden.

Alternative refreshment stops
At the footbridge joining the Regent's Canal is Bow Wharf where you'll find the Fat Cat Café and Bar. This converted builders' yard has outside, daytime seating and a wooden interior with Chesterfield sofas.

☞ Where to go from here
Visit the Ragged School Museum in Copperfield Road, one of 148 schools set up by Dr Barnado, which highlights the history of the East End, with a Victorian schoolroom taster session for children (www.raggedschoolmuseum.org.uk). The Museum in Docklands at West India Quay unlocks the history of London's river, port and people in a spectacular 19th-century warehouse (www.museumindocklands.org.uk).

about the pub

The Crown
223 Grove Road
London E3 5SN
Tel: 020 8981 9998
www.singhboulton.co.uk

DIRECTIONS: at the junction of Grove Road and Old Ford Road (off walk at Point 4). Nearest tube: Mile End

PARKING: none

OPEN: all day; closed Monday lunchtime except Bank Holidays

FOOD: daily

BREWERY/COMPANY: free house

REAL ALE: Pitfield Eco Warrior, Shoreditch Organic Stout, St Peter's Organic Ale

DOGS: welcome inside

Victoria Park to the Isle of Dogs and Greenwich

Explore parks and canals, and cross the Thames.

Mile End Park and Canary Wharf

Tree-lined Mile End Park Green Bridge was built to unite the park, previously bisected by the Mile End Road. The Green Bridge project involved planting 250 trees and 4,000 shrubs.

At 800ft (244m), One Canada Square is Britain's tallest building. Home to the *Telegraph* and *Mirror* newspaper groups, among other tenants, the original iconic tower has been joined by a cluster of other tall office blocks. More than 60,000 people now work on the 86-acre (35ha) estate on the site of the former West India Docks.

the ride

1 Enter **Victoria Park** through the gate adjacent to the pub. At the crossroads continue straight ahead. When you reach **St Mark's Gate**, remain inside the park and turn right, parallel to the canal. At **Three Colt Bridge** drop down on to the tow path. Where the Hertford Union Canal joins the Regent's Canal, squeeze through the gap for bicycles, head up the slope and turn left across the bridge. At **Roman Road** the left-hand tunnel is for cyclists. When you reach the **red sculpture** turn left into the park. The cycle track rejoins the tow path to pass under the railway bridge. Beyond the bridge once again head left into the park before briefly looping back towards the canal at **Mile End Lock**. Follow the path up on to the Green Bridge across Mile End Road. Keep to the cycle route through the park. Use the toucan crossing by **Mile End Stadium** to rejoin the tow path for a brief stretch to

Salmon Lane Lock. At the lock use the ramp provided and turn right along the pavement. The path then bends to the left and goes straight ahead into Salmon Lane, with the tower of **St Anne's Limehouse** ahead.

2 At Commercial Road use the toucan crossing by the former town hall, and continue ahead along **Newell Street**. Beyond the railway bridge the street bends to the left to meet Colt Street. Turn right here. At the crossroads with Narrow Street and Limehouse Causeway continue straight ahead along **Emmett Street**. Keep straight ahead at Milligan Street. Above the Limehouse Link tunnel the route joins the riverside to pass **Canary Wharf Pier**. Cross the bridge over a pumping station outlet, then head up the ramp and remain on the riverside until the derelict remains of **West India Dock Pier**. Turn left into Cuba Street and cross Westferry Road. At the end of Cuba Street join Manilla Street. Turn left into Byng Street and right into Mastmaker Road. At the bend this becomes **Lighterman's Road**. Turn right into Millharbour. Just before the end of the road turn left on to traffic-free **Pepper Street**.

3 When you reach Glengall Bridge cross the drawbridge and turn right, following the edge of **Millwall Docks**. There is an easily missed sign just by the wire fence with turquoise posts. Turn left here and pass under the **Docklands Light Railway**, climbing up the ramp on the other side to join East Ferry Road. Turn right along the road here. By Mudchute Station there is a zebra crossing. Leave the road here and turn left into the park by the entrance to **Mudchute Farm**. There is a ramp marked for cyclists, but the barriers are tricky. The path soon bends to the right to run alongside the disued railway viaduct, emerging next to the **Docklands Light Railway station**.

4 At **Island Gardens station** use the toucan crossing and turn right to join the cycle path on the far side of the road. Almost immediately take a left turn into Ferry Street, then follow the left-hand fork to reach the gates of Island Gardens and the northern entrance to the **Greenwich Foot Tunnel** (lift operates until 7pm Mon–Sat, 5.30pm Sun). You will need to push your bike through the tunnel.

5 When you emerge in Greenwich turn right, past the *Gipsy Moth IV*, and pick up the green surfaced **cycle path** along the riverside. Turn left at Horseferry Place, then take the first right into Thames Street, turning left into Norway Street. Use the pavement to cross **Deptford Creek**, with the multicoloured Laban dance centre to your left. At The Hoy turn right, then follow the green surface of the riverside cycle track past the statue of **Peter the Great**. Continue straight ahead along Borthwick Street. After the cobbled section follow the road round to the left into Watergate Street, and take the first right into Prince Street. Look for the right turn into **Dacca Street**. When you reach Sayes Court Street, bear half-right and negotiate the bollards to take the nameless linking alleyway to reach Grove Street. Just past Dragoon Road turn right into the park, following the **red path**. On the far side of the park use the cycle channel provided to pull your bike up the stairs. Ride through **Pepys Park** to reach the river, turning left along the riverside.

3h30	11 MILES	17.7 KM	LEVEL 123

MAP: OS Explorer 173 London North

START/FINISH: The Victoria Park, Victoria Park Road; grid ref: TQ 361843

TRAILS/TRACKS: well-surfaced tracks

LANDSCAPE: mix of parkland, waterside and urban streets

PUBLIC TOILETS: Victoria Park and Greenwich

TOURIST INFORMATION: Greenwich, tel 0870 608 2000

CYCLE HIRE: Wharf Cycles, 21–23 Westferry Road, E14 8JH, tel 020 7987 2255

THE PUB: The Victoria Park, 360 Victoria Park Road, E9

🛈 Some on-road sections are perhaps unsuitable for younger, less experienced children. A free permit is necessary to cycle along Regent's Canal (www.waterscape.com). Note the closing times for the Greenwich Tunnel lifts. You will have to pay to use the ferry service from Rotherhithe Pier.

Getting to the start

Victoria Park Road is just off the A12 East Cross Road at Hackney Wick. There's free on-street parking around Well Street Common.

Why do this cycle ride?

This ride has it all: parks, canals, a tree-lined bridge, skyscrapers, rivers, tunnels, ferries and much more. Londoners and non-Londoners alike will be amazed by how much there is to see in the East End and Docklands.

Researched and written by: James Hatts

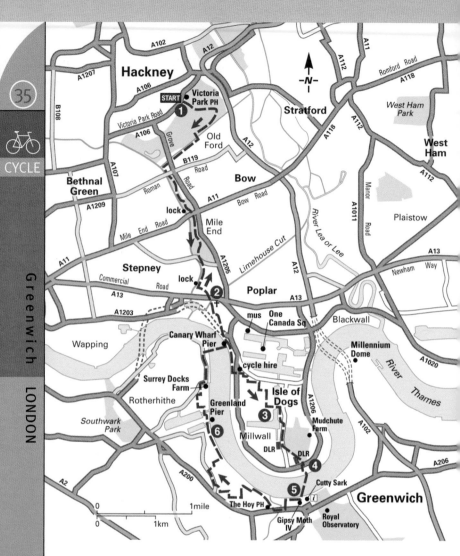

6 At **South Lock** use the lock gates to cross the water, and remain on the riverside past the **Greenland Pier**. Follow the road round to join South Sea Street and cross the bridge. At the end turn left into Finland Street. Very soon there is a right turn on to traffic-free **Bonding Yard Walk**. Just before the underpass turn right into Rotherhithe Street. Bear right to remain on Rotherhithe Street as it converges with

Salter Road. **Surrey Docks Farm** is to your right. At the Hilton Hotel turn right up the main entrance ramp. Access to **Rotherhithe Pier** is through the hotel lobby (bicycles can be wheeled through). Ferries back to Canary Wharf run frequently (to 10.30pm weekdays, to 6.30pm weekends). From Canary Wharf return to Victoria Park via the outward route.

The Victoria Park

about the pub

The Victoria Park
360 Victoria Park Road
London E9 7BT
Tel: 020 8985 0693

DIRECTIONS: The Victoria Park is next to the Queen's Gate entrance to Victoria Park in Victoria Park Road, opposite Well Street Common. Victoria Park Road can be reached from the A12 East Cross Route at Hackney Wick	
PARKING: free on-street parking around Well Street Common, across from the pub	
OPEN: daily; all day	
FOOD: daily; all day (until 5pm Sunday)	
BREWERY/COMPANY: Qs	
REAL ALE: none available	

After a period of closure the Victoria Park has reopened, sporting its bright new décor. With Well Street Common opposite and Victoria Park to the rear, it is situated in a pleasant green corner of South Hackney. The clientele is mixed; a youthful crowd inhabits the games area with the pool tables, while families take advantage of the outside seating. The 'garden' was previously used as a car park and doesn't have much greenery apart from the canopy of trees. Bicycle parking is available directly outside the pub.

Food
The colourful menu has starters such as potato longboats and spicy chicken dippers. Main courses include grilled Cajun chicken and vegetable rigatoni. There are also burgers, wraps and baguettes.

Family facilities
Children are welcome until 7pm. Smaller portions of the main course dishes are available.

Alternative refreshment stops
There are plenty of bars, cafés and restaurants at Canary Wharf and Greenwich.

☛ Where to go from here
The Museum in Docklands (www.museumindocklands.org.uk) unlocks the history of London's river, port and people and is housed in a fascinating early 19th-century warehouse. Exhibits include enormous whale bones and World War Two gas masks, and children can explore the interactive gallery

Mudlarks'. Along the route is the Cutty Sark Clipper Ship, the last and most famous tea-clipper, which broke all records in 1885. The cabins have been reconstructed to show what life at sea was like in the 1870s (www.cuttysark.org.uk). On the Isle of Dogs, stop off at Mudchute Park and Farm, a working farm since 1977, where childrn can see and handle animals, including pigs, goats, horses, guinea pigs and the residential llama.

Across the river to Greenwich

Discover more about the background to Greenwich Mean Time on a walk through Greenwich Park.

Maritime Greenwich

Until the 17th century, captains could tell the ship's position of latitude by the stars and the sun, but longitude was a real problem: they had no way of telling how far east or west a ship was positioned resulting in many wrecks.

Charles II rescued Greenwich after it fell on hard times under Oliver Cromwell. The birthplace of Henry VIII and his daughters Mary I and Elizabeth I, Greenwich was given a Royal Observatory in 1675 to try to provide seafarers with more accurate charts. The first Astronomer Royal was John Flamsteed who took the job at the age of 28. During his 45 years at the observatory, he made more than 50,000 observations. However, he did not arrive at a solution for longitude. When, in 1707, four Royal Navy ships sank off the Isles of Scilly, claiming 2,000 lives. Parliament offered a reward of £20,000 for anyone finding a solution to the longitude problem. It was won – by a clockmaker.

John Harrison (1693–1776) came to London in 1730 with the idea that longitude could be worked out by using the time. His solution was based on the fact that for every 15 degrees travelled eastwards, local time moves one hour ahead. Therefore, if we know the local times at two points on Earth, we can use the difference between them to calculate how far apart those places are in longitude, east or west. This idea was crucial to sailors in the 17th century. The problem was that every minute gained or lost could amount to a error of 15 nautical miles (17.25 miles or 28.9km) so the solution hinged on producing a clock that kept the exact time in turbulent conditions. Harrison made four clocks for this purpose. The first was designed to run consistently, regardless of movement or temperature changes. He made a second clock, then took 19 years to work on the third prototype, the H3. However, it was his fourth, the H4, which clinched the deal.

The most compact, it was the forerunner of all precision watches and provided the basis for an accurate sea chronometer which finally enabled sailors to work out their exact position.

In 1884 it was decided, at an international conference in Washington DC, that Greenwich should become the site of the prime meridian, an imaginary line running north to south, denoting the world's longitudinal zero. This means that every position on Earth is defined by its longitude (distance east or west) from Greenwich.

the walk

1 From **Island Gardens DLR** cross Manchester Road and go up Ferry Road opposite. Turn left into Saunders Ness Road and after a short distance turn into **Island Gardens**. Cross the Thames by the foot tunnel. With the *Cutty Sark* on your left, continue ahead into Greenwich Church Street. Cross the road on the crossing and take the second turning into the market. At the far end turn right and use the crossings to go over the main road before following King William Walk to **Greenwich Park**.

1h45 · **3.5 MILES** · **5.7 KM** · **LEVEL 1 2 3**

2 Enter the park at **St Mary's Gate** and follow the wide path, known as The Avenue, as it swings to the left uphill. Continue ahead, turning left at the toilets to reach the **Royal Observatory** and a superb view over London and the Greenwich Royal Naval College.

3 Retrace your steps, past the Royal Observatory's **Planetarium building** and a café to follow this broad pathway, Blackheath Avenue. Just before Blackheath Gate turn left through some metal gates into the **Flower Garden** and along a path that skirts the edge of a large pond.

View from Greenwich Hill to the Royal Naval College, Queen's House and Canary Wharf

MAP: OS Explorer 161 London South
START/FINISH: Island Gardens DLR station
PATHS: tarmac paths
LANDSCAPE: parkland with panoramic views
PUBLIC TOILETS: in Greenwich Park
TOURIST INFORMATION: Greenwich, tel 0870 608 2000
THE PUB: Trafalgar Tavern, Park Row, SE10

Getting to the start
Island Gardens tube station is on the A1206 Manchester Road on the Isle of Dogs. There is street parking. The station is on the Docklands Light Railway.

Researched and written by:
Leigh Hatts, Deborah King

Greenwich

LONDON

WALK

4 Turn right at the two path junctions before reaching the **exit gates** to the enclosure. Turn left and take the right-hand fork. Continue along this straight path beside a wall.

5 At the next junction take the second path on the left and keep ahead, straight over another set of paths, to reach another junction at which an **oak tree** is protected by railings. This dates from the 12th century and lived to a ripe old age of 700 years. It is said that Anne Boleyn danced around the tree with Henry VIII, and their daughter, Elizabeth, would often play in the hollow trunk of the huge oak.

6 Turn right, downhill, and right again at the next junction on a path that dips and rises. Continue ahead at the next set of paths and leave the park at **Park Row Gate**. Keep ahead along Park Row, past the

what to look for

The Greenwich Foot Tunnel was built in 1902 to link Greenwich with the Isle of Dogs, so workers from south London could get to the docks. The wood-panelled lifts that take you underground were replaced in the 1990s. They are enormous and quite a contrast from the starkness of the foot tunnel. The lift attendants also have use of a small electric heater in winter so, if you're not warm after the 400yd (366m) walk along the foot tunnel, you soon will be.

National Maritime Museum and across Romney Road.

7 At the Trafalgar Tavern turn left along the Thames Path to reach **Greenwich Pier**. Retrace your steps along the **Greenwich Foot Tunnel** to Island Gardens DLR station.

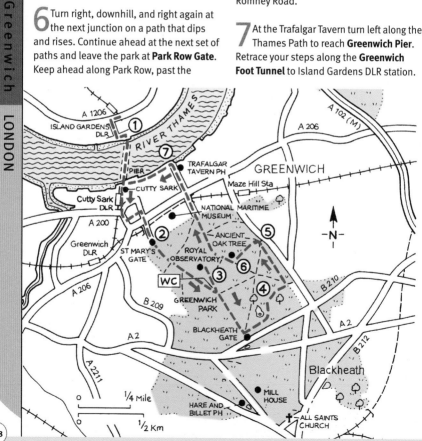

The Trafalgar Tavern

A stunning location by the Thames and a noteworthy history make this an interesting pub to visit. It was built in 1837 to commemorate the 1805 Battle of Trafalgar, Dick Turpin was known to have frequented the pub, and scenes from Dickens' Our Mutual Friend were set here. With the Thames lapping against the walls, the attractive stone building has four elegant, high-ceilinged rooms, including a central bar with old fireplaces, maritime memorabilia, jugs and bottles, a lovely river-view bow window, and a grand, wood-panelled dining room that was famous for its 'whitebait suppers' in the 19th century. Cabinet ministers often travelled downriver from Westminster to relish this speciality. A Greenwich institution.

about the pub

Trafalgar Tavern
Park Row, London SE10 9NW
Tel: 020 8858 2909

DIRECTIONS: beside the Thames, east of Greenwich Pier (on walk at Point 7). Nearest rail: Cutty Sark Gardens DLR	
PARKING: none	
OPEN: daily; all day	
FOOD: daily; all day	
BREWERY/COMPANY: Greenwich Inc	
REAL ALE: Fuller's London Pride, Nelson's Blood	
DOGS: allowed inside	

Food
The menu features fish, including chargrilled sardines and the famous whitebait meals, along with traditional English dishes such as sausages and mash, and lamb with rosemary.

Family facilities
Children are welcome inside. There's a children's menu and high chairs are available.

Alternative refreshment stops
Goddard's Pie House in Greenwich Church Street.

☞ Where to go from here
The National Maritime Museum in the centre of Greenwich has changing and interactive displays that explore Britain's seafaring history (www.nmm.ac.uk). The Royal Observatory in Greenwich Park houses an extensive collection of historic timekeeping, astronomical and navigational instruments. Board the Cutty Sark, the last and most famous tea-clipper, which broke all records in 1885, and learn about life at sea, above and below decks, on its tea/wool routes between China/Australia and Britain (www.cuttysark.org.uk).

WALK

Greenwich LONDON

East from Greenwich along the Thames

Explore the Millennium Dome, the Thames Barrier and Royal Arsenal.

Thames Barrier and Royal Arsenal

The Thames Barrier has been put to use more than 80 times to protect London from flooding. Construction began in 1974 and a decade later the Queen carried out the official opening. More than 80 staff are required to operate and maintain the flood defences. The barrier is made up of ten movable gates positioned end-to-end across the river. It's closed once a month

for testing and maintenance; dates are published on the Environment Agency's website. The Agency estimates that a major flood in central London could cost as much as £30,000 million.

The first ordnance stores at Woolwich were set up in the 16th century by Henry VIII, when gun manufacturing was moved from the City of London to the comparative safety of Woolwich. From the early 1700s Woolwich became the headquarters of the Royal Artillery companies, and a military academy was established soon after. The title Royal Arsenal was granted in 1805 by George III, in recognition of Woolwich's

Across the Thames is the Millennium Dome

2h00 · **6 MILES** · **9.7 KM** · **LEVEL 1 2 3**

importance in ordnance manufacturing. The Royal Ordnance Factory closed in 1967 with the loss of thousands of jobs. The site has now been restored and regenerated into an attractive riverside leisure complex.

the ride

1 If you are starting from the parking at **Cutty Sark Gardens** wheel your bike along the riverside walk to the **Cutty Sark** pub and turn right along Ballast Quay, then bear right into Pelton Road. At the Royal Standard pub turn left into Christchurch Way. As you approach the entrance to the **Alcatel complex,** turn right into Mauritius Road. On reaching Blackwall Lane turn left into the bus lane. Just before the traffic lights take the **cycle path** on the left which runs along the pavement of Tunnel Avenue. At the footbridge look for the **green surfaced track** on the left.

2 Cross the footbridge and turn left into Boord Street. At **Millennium Way**, join the cycle path directly ahead. At West Parkside continue straight on and when you reach the riverside, turn right. Just past the colourful buildings of Greenwich Millennium Village you will reach the **Greenwich Peninsula Ecology Park**.

3 The outer boardwalk is open at all times and considerate cyclists are welcome. Continue along the riverside path, which turns inland to skirt the **Greenwich Yacht Club**'s fenced enclosure. Remain on the riverside past the aggregate recycling works. At the end of that section, stay on the street called **Riverside**, with the large Sainsbury's depot to your right. Look out for

MAP: OS Explorer 162 Greenwich & Gravesend

START/FINISH: Cutty Sark pub, Ballast Quay; grid ref: TQ 389782. Pay parking at Cutty Sark Gardens

TRAILS/TRACKS: largely surfaced cycle lanes, some cobbled streets

LANDSCAPE: industrial and waterside

PUBLIC TOILETS: close to Woolwich Ferry

TOURIST INFORMATION: Greenwich, tel 0870 608 2000

CYCLE HIRE: none locally

THE PUB: Cutty Sark, Greenwich, SE10

🛑 This ride includes some busy on-road sections where you may prefer to dismount

Getting to the start

The Cutty Sark pub is north east of Greenwich town centre. Lassell Street leads to Ballast Quay from Trafalgar Road (A206). On-street metered parking is limited to 2 hours; Greenwich Council underground parking at Cutty Sark Gardens is a short walk or ride.

Why do this cycle ride?

In the space of just 3 miles (4.8km) of riverside there is at least a millennium's worth of London's industrial, military and seafaring heritage to explore, from Maritime Greenwich to the Royal Arsenal, via the engineering feat of the Thames Barrier and the unmistakable landmark of the Millennium Dome.

Researched and written by: James Hatts

the remains of old dockside railway tracks on your left. At **Anchor and Hope Lane** take the off-road path straight ahead.

4 On reaching the **Thames Barrier**, the green-surfaced route around the complex is well-signed and easy to follow. At the former Thames Barrier Arms pub, go straight ahead along the narrow and slightly overgrown path. There is a steep slope up to the crossing at **Woolwich Church Street**. Turn left along the road here. When you reach the roundabout, take the second exit (Ruston Road). Look for the left turn where Ruston Road heads towards the river. Turn left here and left again at **Harlinger Road**. At the T-junction turn right, then right again.

5 A sign asks cyclists to dismount for the 40yd (37m) section between the road and the riverside. When you rejoin the riverside opposite the **Tate & Lyle works**

on the north bank, turn right. When the pedestrian route uses steps to cross a wall, the cycle path heads inland where there is a ramp and returns to the **riverside**.

6 At the canons on the riverside turn inland past the **Clockhouse Community Centre**. At Leda Road make your way up the slope to join Woolwich Church Street. You may prefer to dismount and push your bike to reach the **Woolwich Free Ferry**. At the Ferry Approach look for the cycle signs by the ambulance station. Pass the Waterfront Leisure Centre and the entrance to the **Woolwich Foot Tunnel**. Continue along the riverside to **Royal Arsenal Pier**, where a large piazza provides access to the revitalised Royal Arsenal complex, including the Firepower Museum. From here it is possible to cycle inland to the shops and services of Woolwich town centre before you return to **Greenwich**.

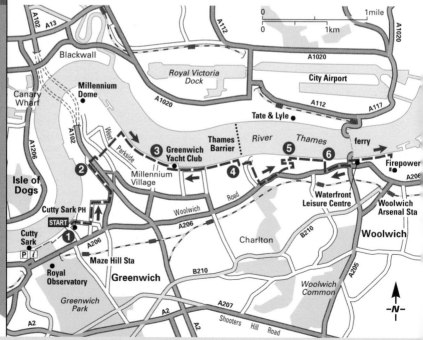

The Cutty Sark

Originally the Union Tavern, this 1695 waterside pub was renamed when the world-famous tea-clipper was dry-docked upriver in 1954. It is part of an attractive row of historic buildings surrounded by modern developments. Inside you will find low beams, creaking floorboards, dark panelling and, from large bow windows in the upstairs bar, commanding views of the Thames, the clusters of skyscrapers at Canary Wharf and the unmistakable Millennium Dome. There is splendid riverside seating on the waterside terrace across the narrow cobbled street.

Food

A permanent menu of door-step sandwiches, jacket potatoes and ploughman's lunches is backed up with daily specials such as chicken breast stuffed with brie, feta cheese and olive salad. A separate board lists fish and seafood dishes such as lemon pepper tiger prawns with rice and salad. Desserts include chocolate temptation cheesecake. Sunday roast lunches are also available.

Family facilities

Children are welcome inside the pub. The riverside terrace is also ideal for families.

Alternative refreshment stops

There is a terrace café at the Thames Barrier and a café at the Royal Arsenal.

☛ Where to go from here

Step on board the Cutty Sark, the fastest tea clipper ever; built in 1869, she once sailed 363 miles (584km) in a single day (www.cuttysark.org.uk). Put science into action with touch-screen displays and be awed by the big guns at Firepower – the Royal Artillery Museum, where the history of artillery from stone shot to shell is explained (www.firepower.org.uk). At the Thames Barrier Learning and Information Centre find out more about the world's largest movable flood barrier, the flood threat of the Thames and the construction of this £535 million project (www.environment-agency.gov.uk).

about the pub

Cutty Sark
4–7 Ballast Quay, Greenwich London SE10 9PD
Tel: 020 8858 3146

DIRECTIONS: see Getting to the start	
PARKING: metered roadside parking	
OPEN: daily; all day	
FOOD: daily; all day (until 6pm at weekends)	
BREWERY/COMPANY: free house	
REAL ALE: Fuller's London Pride, Greene King Old Speckled Hen, Adnams Broadside	

Along Regent's Canal

Explore the Regent's Canal from the Thames to the Islington Tunnel.

The Ragged School Museum and Angel Islington

The ride passes the Ragged School Museum, which is housed in three canalside warehouses, originally built to store lime juice and general provisions, but later used by Dr Barnardo to house the largest ragged school in London. The Museum was opened in 1990 to bring the unique history of this school to life. In a re-created classroom of the period you can experience how children in the Victorian East End were taught. Poor local children received a free education, breakfast, dinner and help finding their first job. The warehouses were used as a day school until 1908, and evening classes and Sunday schools continued until 1915.

The Angel Islington is instantly familiar to millions of people who have played the British version of the Monopoly board game. The area of Islington takes its name from an inn that once stood here. In the early 1800s it became a coaching inn; the first staging post outside the City of London. A local landmark, the inn was mentioned by Charles Dickens in Oliver Twist. The site of the pub is now occupied by a bank. Angel underground station boasts the longest escalators in Western Europe, with a vertical rise of 90ft (27m) and a length of 197ft (60m).

the ride

1 Turn left along Narrow Street. At the entrance to **Limehouse Basin** continue

straight ahead; cycling is not permitted on the tow path here. At Colt Street turn left, then turn left again into Newell Street and follow it round to the right under the railway viaduct. **St Anne's Limehouse** is a striking landmark to the right.

2 At the former **Limehouse Town Hall** use the toucan crossing to reach the other side of both Commercial Road and the Canal. Use the cycle lane to join Salmon Lane. At **Rhodeswell Street** the route

One of several locks passed along the route

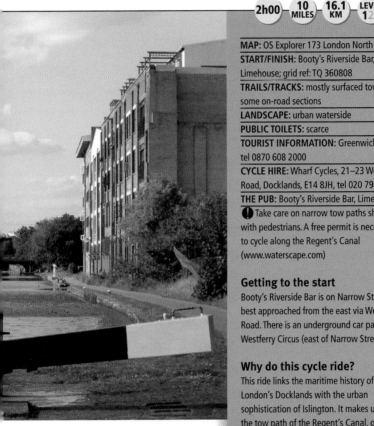

2h00 **10 MILES** **16.1 KM** **LEVEL 123**

MAP: OS Explorer 173 London North
START/FINISH: Booty's Riverside Bar, Limehouse; grid ref: TQ 360808
TRAILS/TRACKS: mostly surfaced tow path; some on-road sections
LANDSCAPE: urban waterside
PUBLIC TOILETS: scarce
TOURIST INFORMATION: Greenwich, tel 0870 608 2000
CYCLE HIRE: Wharf Cycles, 21–23 Westferry Road, Docklands, E14 8JH, tel 020 7987 2255
THE PUB: Booty's Riverside Bar, Limehouse
🛈 Take care on narrow tow paths shared with pedestrians. A free permit is necessary to cycle along the Regent's Canal (www.waterscape.com)

Getting to the start
Booty's Riverside Bar is on Narrow Street, best approached from the east via Westferry Road. There is an underground car park at Westferry Circus (east of Narrow Street).

Why do this cycle ride?
This ride links the maritime history of London's Docklands with the urban sophistication of Islington. It makes use of the tow path of the Regent's Canal, opened in 1820 to link the Grand Union Canal's Paddington Arm with the River Thames. The tow path is an ideal route for cyclists to skirt the centre of London, free from traffic.

Researched and written by: James Hatts

continues straight ahead, leaving the traffic behind until Islington.

3 Don't take the footbridge over the canal, but turn right and use the ramp to join the tow path at **Salmon Lane Lock**. Follow the tow path under the railway and past the solitary remaining chimney. Ignore the National Cycle Network sign inviting you to head inland at Mile End Stadium and remain on the tow path. Just past the **Ben Jonson Road bridge** is the Ragged School

Museum's tow path café which you may be lucky enough to find open. The overhanging **warehouses** on the west side of the canal are a feature of this section. Beyond Mile End Lock look for the **water feature** on the right-hand side.

4 A bridge carries the tow path over the junction between the Regent's Canal and the Hertford Union Canal. Beyond **Old Ford Lock** there is some respite from the post-industrial landscape with a pleasantly green section alongside **Victoria Park**. Soon a **gasometer** looms ahead and the tow path passes under the road and railway.

5 The tow path then crosses a bridge over the entrance to Kingsland Basin. Beyond **Sturt's Lock** there are some larger permanently moored boats – these are converted Thames lighters that form part of the adjacent photographic studio complex. **City Road Basin** can be seen on the left, closely followed by City Road Lock. The entrance of **Islington Tunnel** soon looms.

6 Take the ramp up to road level. Head straight up **Duncan Street** to sample the attractions of The Angel Islington before tackling the return ride to Limehouse.

A sculpture in Mile End Park

Booty's Riverside Bar

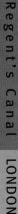

Booty's Riverside Bar has been a pub since the late 1970s – the 18th-century building was once a barge-builders' store. Formerly known as the Waterman's Arms, it is now a mix between a traditional-style riverside pub and a wine bar, but has an atmosphere more akin to a friendly local pub. The single bar is long and narrow, with a lower level laid out for dining and with fine river views. Those who prefer to dine al fresco will have to settle for a table on the pavement side. There are bicycle racks directly opposite the bar.

Food
The menu offers steak and kidney pie, bangers and mash, a variety of ploughman's meals and much more; perhaps a delicious warming soup or a dressed crab salad. Desserts include apple pie and ice-cream.

about the pub

Booty's Riverside Bar
94A Narrow Street,
Limehouse
London E14 8DQ
Tel: 020 7987 8343

DIRECTIONS: in Narrow Street, best approached from the east via Westferry Road

PARKING: on-street pay-and-display on Narrow Street

OPEN: daily; all day

FOOD: daily; all day

BREWERY/COMPANY: free house

REAL ALE: Tetley, Bass

Family facilities
Children are welcome inside the bar.

Alternative refreshment stops
There's a good canal-side café at the Ragged School Museum and a full range of refreshment opportunities at the Angel.

☛ Where to go from here
Take a look at The Wapping Project, an international arts venue housed in a restored Grade II-listed hydraulic power station. You'll find contemporary gallery spaces, performance areas, a bookshop and a café. Head east along the Thames to visit the Tower Bridge Exhibition and learn more about how the world's famous bridge works and the history behind it. You can enjoy stunning views from the walkways situated 148ft (45m) above the Thames and visit the original Victorian turbines (www.towerbridge.org.uk).

Around Wanstead Park

Through Wanstead Park, where Robert Dudley, Earl of Leicester, entertained Elizabeth I.

Wanstead Park

The surprising thing about Wanstead Park in east London is that, despite its close proximity to the North Circular road, the distant hum of traffic is really only noticeable from the northern side of the park. This is a lovely walk, enchanting even, for it traces the outline of the ornamental waters and passes the Grotto and Temple. No wonder Elizabeth I kept returning.

Wanstead has been associated with royalty ever since 1553 when Queen Mary, a Roman Catholic, broke her journey here from Norwich to meet her sister, Princess Elizabeth, a Protestant, who rode out to Wanstead accompanied by hundreds of knights on horseback. The estate had belonged to Sir Giles Heron but, because he would not renounce his Catholic beliefs, Henry VIII (the girls' father) took it from him. After Mary's death, Elizabeth became Queen – she was just 25 years old. The estate at Wanstead then belonged to Robert Dudley, the Earl of Leicester, who had enlarged and improved the mansion. The two became very close and Dudley held some extremely lavish parties for his royal guest. In 1578 Elizabeth stayed in Wanstead for five days and no doubt would have spent some time walking in the wonderful grounds.

When Queen Elizabeth died, James I succeeded her. In 1607 he spent the autumn in Wanstead. The manor was later sold to Sir James Mildmay. Unfortunately, as Mildmay was one of the judges at the trial of Charles I, which led to Charles' execution, the manor was taken from the family after the Restoration and handed to the Crown. In 1667 Sir Josiah Child (whose family were the first private bankers in England) bought the manor and made huge improvements. Later, his son, Sir Richard, replaced the manor house and landscaped the gardens. Constructed using Portland stone, the front of the new mansion had a portico of six Corinthian columns. The building was considered one of the finest in the country, even rivalling Blenheim Palace. The Grotto was erected and the ornamental waters and lakes were also designed at this time. But why, you might ask, is there no mansion today? The blame lies chiefly with Catherine Tilney-Long, who inherited the extremely valuable property in 1794. Despite no shortage of admiring males, she married a gambling man, who took just ten years to blow her entire fortune. To pay off her husband's debts Catherine auctioned the contents of the house and, because a buyer could not be found for the house itself, the magnificent property was pulled down and sold in separate lots. Fortunately for us, despite this sad tale of decline, the wonderful grounds can still be enjoyed.

the walk

1 Turn left outside Wanstead tube station into **The Green**, which becomes St Mary's Avenue. At the end, by **St Mary's Church**, turn left into Overton Drive. After the Bowls and Golf Club turn right into **The Warren Drive**. (The building on the right, before the road bends, was once the stable block and coach house to Wanstead House.)

| 3h00 | 4.75 MILES | 7.7 KM | LEVEL 1 123 |

WALK

2 At the T-junction turn left and, almost immediately, enter **Wanstead Park** through a gateway opposite. Continue ahead down wooded Florrie's Hill to reach the **ornamental water**. Follow the path to the left of the water and continue ahead as it runs to the right of the River Roding.

3 After another 0.25 mile (400m) the path swings sharply to the left round an area known as the **Fortifications**, once a group of eight islands used for storing ammunition for duck-shooting and now a bird sanctuary. Soon after this the path traces the outline of a section of the water shaped like a finger. To your left are the steep banks of the **River Roding**.

4 At a meeting of paths turn right to continue alongside the water. When the path bends to the left, you will see the **Grotto** ahead.

Top and below: Wanstead Park

MAP: OS Explorer 174 Epping Forest & Lee Valley

START/FINISH: Wanstead tube station; grid ref: TQ 406882

PATHS: good tracks

LANDSCAPE: woodland and waterside meadow

PUBLIC TOILETS: none on route

TOURIST INFORMATION: Ilford, tel 020 8708 2420

THE PUB: The George, Wanstead, E11

Getting to the start

Wanstead is on the A12 between Leytonstone and Redbridge. There is street parking in St Mary's Avenue near Wanstead tube station, which can also be reached via the Central Line.

Researched and written by:
Leigh Hatts, Deborah King

Wanstead

LONDON

what to look for

Spare a moment to gaze at the fairytale Grotto, which was overlooked when Wanstead House was pulled down. Now a Grade II-listed building, it was encrusted with shells, stalactites, crystals and pebbles, many of which were found in the lake after a fire damaged the Grotto in 1884. The chamber had a domed roof and a stained-glass window and it was accessible by a set of steps from the lake.

5 At the T-junction turn right. At the end of the water turn right again, to cross a **footbridge**; then take the left-hand fork towards a field. Bear left to follow the trees on the left to reach a T-junction by a tea hut facing the **Heronry Pond**. Turn left to reach a gate at a road.

6 Immediately turn right to pick up a path leading to Heronry Pond, which narrows and passes over a mound. Where the path divides take the right fork nearest the water each time. On reaching a **firm gravel path** at the end of the pond turn right.

7 The path bears right round the end of the pond to run along the far side of the water and reach a **metal gate**. Go through this and take a left-hand fork to join a wide, grassy track lined with sweet chestnut trees. At the front of the **Temple** take the well-defined path along the right side which runs gently downhill.

8 When the path enters a wood turn left on a **gravel path** which runs down to water near the Grotto. Follow this path as it hugs the water's edge. Turn next left up **Florrie's Hill** to retrace your steps back to Wanstead tube.

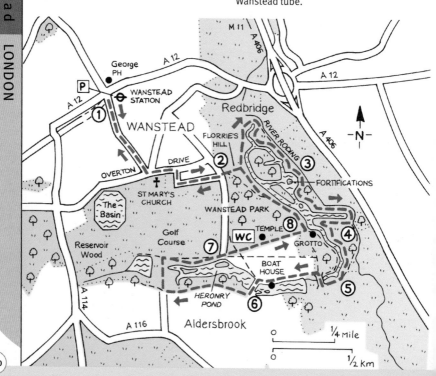

The George

This rather grand Victorian corner building is on a leafy street with wide pavements opposite Wanstead tube. Unlike many pubs in the Wetherspoon chain, The George has always been a pub and, as a result, has a comfortable, more intimate feel about the place. Expect an impressive marble porch, partly frosted windows and a smartly refurbished interior, with bookshelves lining the walls and pictures of famous 'Georges' and of Old Wanstead. The excellent range of real ales from independent breweries changes regularly.

Food

Snacks include paninis, wraps, sandwiches and jacket potatoes, while main meals include salads, pasta dishes, fish and chips, sausages and mash, vegetarian moussaka, and rump steak with peppercorn sauce. There are also Sunday roast lunches.

Family facilities

Children are welcome inside and you will find an extensive children's menu, including a child's portion of roast lunch on Sundays. There is also a sheltered patio with trees and benches.

Alternative refreshment stops

The tea hut in Wanstead Park is often open during the day.

☞ Where to go from here

St Mary's Church in Overton Drive is where Elizabeth I worshipped during her many visits to Wanstead. Now Grecian in style and cased with white Portland stone, it has four imposing columns. The church was designed by Thomas Hardwick, who was also associated with the building of Somerset House. You'll find a monument to the memory of Sir Josiah Child in the chancel.

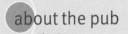

about the pub

The George
159 High Street, Wanstead
London E11 2RL
Tel: 020 8989 2921
www.jdwetherspoon.co.uk

DIRECTIONS: the pub is at the start/finish of the walk	
PARKING: 20	
OPEN: daily; all day	
FOOD: daily; all day	
BREWERY/COMPANY: JD Wetherspoon	
REAL ALE: changing range of beers from micro-breweries	
DOGS: not allowed inside	

Chislehurst

Chislehurst Common

Willett's daylight saving

The inventor of British Summer Time lived in Chislehurst. William Willett was a builder by trade. On this walk you will pass his house, Cedars, which he built himself. It was while out riding in nearby Petts Wood one day that he was inspired by an idea to increase the hours of light in the day 'to improve health and happiness'. He soon became obsessed with the concept. In 1907 he circulated a pamphlet around Parliament and town councils, which argued that the many hours of light wasted while people slept in the mornings should be transferred to the evenings. Although it was met with considerable opposition, a Daylight Saving Bill was introduced in 1909. However, it would take another seven years to pass. Had it not been for World War One, Willett's idea may have remained on the shelf but, in

1916, a committee was set up to investigate ways of saving fuel. Consequently Willett's suggestion was given serious consideration. Indeed, it was introduced as a wartime economy measure in many countries. Sadly, William Willett never lived to see his scheme put into effect as he died in 1915. However, his summer-time legacy lives on and today Britain keeps Greenwich Mean Time (GMT) in winter and British Summer Time (BST) in summer.

Another former Chislehurst resident played an historic role in world affairs, and the course of history in the 20th century would have been very different had Napoleon III's son, Eugene, the French Prince Imperial, married Beatrice, the daughter of Queen Victoria. The two had become friends but he chose an army career. After training at Woolwich Barracks he went to war in South Africa to fight against the Zulus – he died, it is said, from one of 17 spear wounds to his body. The golf clubhouse near the beginning of the walk was once home to Napoleon III and his wife, Eugenie. Nathaniel Strode, a local man, lent them the building, which was then a private house, when they were exiled from France in 1871. When Napoleon III died in 1873 his body was laid to rest in a chapel at the side of St Mary's Church, before finally being buried at Farnborough in Hampshire.

the walk

1 Walk down Chislehurst High Street, past **Prick End Pond**, cross the road and turn right into Prince Imperial Road. Follow this as it passes a row of large houses and, 50yds (46m) further on, the Methodist church. Where the houses end, take the **bridle path** to the right, running through the trees parallel to the road. When you cross Wilderness Road look left to see the **memorial to Eugene**, the French Prince Imperial.

2 Just past the golf clubhouse is **William Willett's Cedars**, built in 1893 and now identified by a blue plaque. Cross the road and walk up Watts Lane to the left of the **cricket ground**. About 150yds (137m) further on, after a field, is a crossroads. In a few paces take the narrow, tarmac path towards **St Nicholas Church**. Cross a road to visit the churchyard. Leave by the lychgate opposite the porch.

3 Walk down Hawkwood Lane to the left of **The Tiger's Head** pub. After St Mary's Church and a series of school buildings, the road bends to the left to become **Botany Bay**

Willett Memorial

2h00 · **3.5** MILES · **5.7** KM · **LEVEL 1 2 3**

MAP: OS Explorer 162 Greenwich & Gravesend

START/FINISH: Queen's Head at the end of Chislehurst Hight Street; grid ref: TQ 439 708

PATHS: footpaths, field edges and bridle paths

LANDSCAPE: common and woodland

PUBLIC TOILETS: none on route

TOURIST INFORMATION: Swanley, tel 01322 614660

THE PUB: The Tiger's Head, Chislehurst

❶ The section on the Hawkwood Estate may be muddy in places, especially in winter

Getting to the start

Chislehurst is on the A208 between Mottingham and Orpington. The car park is off the High Street, part of the A208, near the Queen's Head. Buses run from Mottingham Station.

Researched and written by:
Leigh Hatts, Deborah King

WALK

Chislehurst LONDON

Lane. Continue ahead but, when you see a waymark and a National Trust sign, take the footpath on the left into the **Hawkwood Estate**, keeping to the right of the central fence. The path descends through woodland and along a boardwalk that skirts the edge of a pond. It then climbs steadily alongside a field (which may contain sheep). At the top is a fine view of **Petts Wood**.

4 At a T-junction turn left into the woodland and at the next junction in just a few yards go right. At a clearing go left to follow the bridle path until you reach **St Paul's Cray Road**. (To visit the Willett memorial keep ahead at the clearing and take the second right.) Cross the road, turn left and take the path running parallel to the road. After 500yds (457m) the path emerges from the woodland to pass in front of houses and cross the end of **Bull Lane**. Keep ahead along the **Royal Parade**

what to look for

As you walk along the tarmac path towards St Nicholas Church notice the sunken area of grass to the left. This is the remains of a cockpit, used for cock fighting – a once-popular sport that was eventually banned in England in 1834.

shopping street and stay on the pavement as it bears right. Note the village sign depicting Elizabeth I knighting Thomas Walsingham in 1597. Cross Bromley Lane.

5 Take a footpath on the left of **Kemnal Road** opposite. Continue along a wide track through the common. At a pond on the right, cross the road and follow a footpath diagonally opposite through some trees. Continue over grass to **Chislehurst High Street**, back to the start.

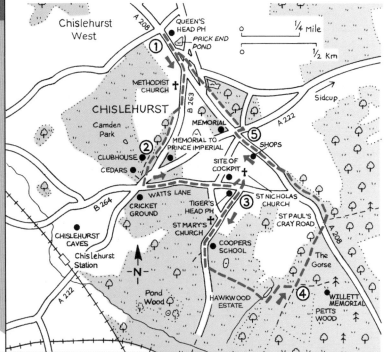

The Tiger's Head

The Tiger's Head is an attractive, two-storey, shuttered pub opposite the historic parish church in this leafy London suburb. Although much modernised over the years, the refurbished interior retains plenty of charm and character, with beamed ceilings, cosy corners and old prints on the walls. The big, paved rear garden has benches and a summer marquee. Note the unusual and impressive pub sign – a huge tiger's head.

about the pub

The Tiger's Head
Watts Lane, Chislehurst
Kent BR7 5PJ
Tel: 020 8467 3070

DIRECTIONS: at the junction of Watts Lane and Hawkwood Lane opposite the church (on walk at Point 3)

PARKING: 10

OPEN: daily, all day

FOOD: daily; all day

BREWERY/COMPANY: Chef & Brewer

REAL ALE: Greene King Old Speckled Hen and Young's Special

DOGS: allowed in the garden only

Food
Bar snacks and main meals feature chicken liver and smoked bacon salad, steak and kidney pudding, whole grilled sea bass, asparagus, pea and mint risotto and, for pudding, ice-creams and banana toffee crumble.

Family facilities
Children are only allowed in the garden.

Alternative refreshment stops
The Bull in Royal Parade or the Queen's Head at the start/finish of the walk.

☞ Where to go from here
Chislehurst Caves (near the railway station) runs lamp-lit tours of a labyrinth of tunnels, spanning more than 20 miles (32km), that were carved from the rocks 8,000 years ago. They have been a druidical base, a wartime air-raid shelter, a film location for Doctor Who, and legendary rock guitarist Jimi Hendrix played to 3,000 fans here in 1967 (www.chislehurstcaves.co.uk).

Acknowledgements

The Automobile Association would like to thank the following photographers and photo library for their assistance in the preparation of this book.

Photolibrary.com front cover b.
Rebecca Harris 16, 19, 23, 27, 31, 39, 43, 51, 52, 59, 60, 63, 79, 87, 91, 103, 115; James Hatts 32/3, 35, 40/1, 42, 43, 44/5, 45, 47, 53, 55, 67, 68, 69, 71, 72, 73, 75, 80/1, 83, 87, 92, 93, 95, 104/5, 107. 140, 143, 144, 145, 147, 155, 163, 164/5. 166. 167; Leigh Hatts 99, 111, 119, 123, 131, 139, 148, 151, 153, 159, 160, 169t, 169b, 171, 173, 175.

The following photographs are held in the Automobile Association's own Photo Library (AA World Travel Library) and were taken by the following photographers:

Malc Birkitt 141; E A Bowness 12; Max Jourdan front cover ccl, 117, 120, 128, 129, 133; Paul Kenward 49, 136/7; Tom Mackie 15; Simon McBride 101t, 106, 121; S & O Mathews 29b, 36/7; John Miller 8/9, 21, 37; Robert Mort 9, 20, 61, 64/5, 65; Barry Smith 57; Tony Souter 14b; Rick Strange 89; James Tims front cover cr, 77t, 85t, 85b, 113, 135, 160; Richard Turpin 109t, 112, 134; Martin Trelawny 29t, 33, 88, 101b, 109b, 126; Wyn Voysey front cover cl, 13, 14t, 116, 127, 137, 157; Peter Wilson 126; Gregory Wrona 4, 48/9. 77b, 98, 172.